"Books on Internet Ma~~~  overload, but Scott has ~~~ the concepts and telling ~~~ exactly what you need to know in a step-by-step, fun, and entertaining way! *80/20 Internet Lead Generation* is the skinny on exactly what you need to know if you want to use the Internet to get your phone ringing!"

—Kim Garst
BoomSocial.net

"Scott Dennison's *80/20 Internet Lead Generation* shows readers who need effective Search Engine Optimization (SEO) what works, what doesn't, and why.

"He kills the excuses for not getting your website seen by your ideal audience and decimates the phony guru-experts who are great at selling unworkable programs that only take your money."

—Tom Justin
CEO, Center Mass Communications, LLC, TomJustin.com

"Lead generation and customer acquisition is the lifeblood of any business. This book will challenge you to leap beyond your current comfort level of marketing and stand up and be heard on the Internet. *80/20 Internet Lead Generation* is filled with valuable insights to growing your business as well as which pitfalls to look out for in the cyber world. If you want to strengthen your business exposure on the Internet, you'll discover a great friend in this book."

—Jim Britt
Author, *Do This. Get Rich – For Entrepreneurs*

"Finally, plain English on Internet marketing for business owners who want the truth and not tech-speak. Read this book and I promise your marketing will never be the same."

—Marguerite Inscoe
B2B Inbound Marketing Ninja, ReLaunchUOff.com

"*80/20 Internet Lead Generation,* by Scott Dennison, is like going out for a drink (or lunch) with a friend in the industry. This book gives you straight on what you need to do to grow your business and attract your ideal customer.

"It's filled with quick, entertaining stories and Dennison's tone is delightfully conversational. His humor makes marketing – a dreaded subject for most business owners – much more palatable and easy to understand. He tells you what needs to be done and makes suggestions on what to look for if you decide to hire the task out.

"The book is a quick read, targeted to business people who *aren't* marketers, to help them make sense of the ever-changing world of SEO and marketing and it does that well."

—Christina R. Green
Professional Writer, christinargreen.com

"Time and again, Scott Dennison has delivered the leads others only promised. Whether you want to do the work yourself, or if you just want to be a more educated client of an outside marketing firm, this book will help you understand what it really takes for online marketing to make your phone ring."

—Dov Gordon
Alchemist Entrepreneur, DovGordon.net

"Given that more than half the buying cycle is complete before you get to talk to your potential client, what Scott Dennison is sharing in *80/20 Internet Lead Generation* is CRUCIAL in today's digital economy! He knows what he's talking about, having been in the proverbial trenches since nearly the beginning of 'the web,' and he's got the actionable clues on what's coming for Web 3.0. To position your business platform properly, this is a comprehensive 'how-to' guide from someone who has his thumb on the mouse!"

—Lynn Scheurell
Business Catalyst, MyCreativeCatalyst.com

"Scott A Dennison, in his new book, *80/20 Internet Lead Generation*, removes the fog created by today's marketers about what works and what doesn't work. He presents readers with a handful of ideas, tips, and actionable strategies that any business owner can accomplish. As someone who's built a very powerful online business through a lot of trial and error, I wish this roadmap would have been available to me years ago."

—Dr. Tony Alessandra
CEO, Assessments24x7.com, and author,
People Smart In Business

"*80/20 Internet Lead Generation* was an excellent read, filled with lots of very useful info that people can, and should, use immediately. I'm looking forward to its general release, so I can share it with the Contractors I work with because, if it helps them as much as it's helped me, it'll be a great investment for them! I would highly recommend this book to any business owner who wants to make the most of their marketing efforts."

—John Browne
GM, Roof-A-Cide, Roof-A-Cide.com

"I met Scott over a decade ago. We also share the same mentor in Jim Rohn – a man who had much wisdom and integrity and left this world a much better place. Knowing Scott worked with this Mentor and is a friend leaves no doubt the wisdom he brings to the table – and his ability to impact others' lives, as Jim Rohn did. Jim always said you would become as successful as the five people you surround yourself with. Scott would be one of those five valuable people, in my book.

"Scott's book is for any business owner who is trying to make sense of online marketing and needs a guide with a plan that works."

—Patrick Dougher
DoerTV.com

"Throughout my reading of Scott Dennison's *80/20 Internet Lead Generation*, which is truly a 'user-friendly Manual,' I found myself recalling a quotation from Zig Ziglar that we shared in our first meeting and as we got to know one another beyond our respective businesses: 'You can get everything in life that you want if you help enough others get what they want.'

"I have seen this theme repeat itself in all areas of your life, Scott – and now in this book.

"Scott's *80/20 Internet Lead Generation* has special appeal to me for three specific reasons:

"**Structure:** Teaching points are succinctly laid out in a highlighted box at the beginning of each chapter and then reviewed at the end of each chapter. This is most helpful to me and will be to readers like me who have ADD and/or Dyslexia. For the general audience, this makes for easy review and note-taking.

"**Content:** Again, on this front, Scott has over-delivered. He's provided the distillation of his work in such a manner that the reader could go forth on his or her own to create a very successful Internet business.

"**One Stop Shop:** Could you get this material other places? Yes – and definitely no. How much time would one spend in searching and curating the material contained in this one source? Simply factor in the value of your time and you'll realize you're losing time, money, and peace of mind by turning anywhere else.

"Do yourself and your business a favor. Get this book, a highlighter, and a notepad!"

—**Virgil Beasley**
Psy.D., <u>Founder</u>. **livingwell60plus.org**

"With so many Internet marketing gimmicks, it's hard to decipher what's real. We've tried most everything, hired consultants, and spent a lot of money in the process – only to be disappointed. Finally! Someone reveals tangible and measurable strategies that will make your phone ring! Scott is a mentor to Internet marketing consultants worldwide and the secrets he shares in his must-read book, *80/20 Internet Lead Generation*, are usually reserved for private sessions. You will want to have a pen and paper handy to take notes as you devour this book!"

—Jason Drenner
Partner, Custom LED Supply,
and CEO, Uprise Marketing Group

"In his book, *80/20 Internet Lead Generation*, Scott gives you the insight and wisdom only a person of great insight and dedication to a craft can, because he's that and more."

—Mark Battiato
Co-Founder, Growth Into Greatness Institute,
greatnessinstitute.com

80/20 Internet Lead Generation

How a few simple, profitable strategies can lead to marketplace domination

Scott A. Dennison

Foreword by Perry Marshall

Publisher, LifePath Books
Graphics and Design, Corena Golliver, Golliver Media
Editing and Production Coordination: Alan R. Bechtold

This publication is designed to provide accurate and authoritative
information in regard to the subject matter covered. It is sold with the
understanding that the publisher is not engaged in rendering legal,
accounting, or other professional services. If legal advice or other expert
assistance is required, the services of a competent professional person
should be sought.

Printed in the United States of America.

I want to say "thanks" to those who have influenced me along the path to getting this book written.

First, I'd like to acknowledge my Lord and Savior, Jesus Christ, for saving me so many years ago and for loving me in all those times when I was unlovable.

Next, I'd like to thank my mentor, the late Jim Rohn, for helping me see possibilities for a better life and for asking me difficult life questions and forcing me to answer them.

I'd also like to thank my parents, Joel and (the late) Elizabeth Dennison. Your influence on me shows more and more the longer I'm around.

Thank you to Alan Bechtold, of LifePath Books, for helping me turn a mountain of my writings into a book that I'm proud to say is mine. Your dedication and skill is really evident.

Finally, to "The Brown-eyed Girl," Hilda Dennison, thank you for being my companion and friend for these last many years. Your love and support in good (and not so good) times and the laughter and fun we've shared mean so much to me.

—Scott A. Dennison

Contents

Foreword..xiii

Introduction..xvii

Chapter One..1

Would You Like a Slurpee™ with that SEO?...........................2

Lying Liars Who Pour Out Lies..7

The Results You Seek are There to be Had.............................13

Chapter Two..17

Internet Business Lead Generation is a *Lot* More than SEO...18

Chapter Three...39

Nailing Down the Ideal Client...40

Chapter Four...53

Defining Your USP...54

NO Soup for You!..59

Chapter Five..69

Generating Effective, Targeted Keywords............................70

Chapter Six...81

PPC Landing Page Concepts...82

Chapter Seven...99

Designing Your Website to Generate *and* Convert Leads.....100

Chapter Eight..**109**

SEO Part One: Optimizing the Right Content.........................110

Chapter Nine...**123**

SEO Part Two: Professional Back-Link Campaigns.............124

Chapter Ten...**135**

Checking Your Results...136

Chapter Eleven **145**

Ongoing Considerations and the Future............................146

Quality, Relevant Content Is Key 148

5 Keys To Successful Social SEO...................................156

Everything is Going Mobile 158

Conclusion 163

What BS! 171

Resources 177

About the Author...179

Foreword

by Perry Marshall

Author, *Ultimate Guide to Google AdWords*
and *80/20 Sales & Marketing*

One of the worst things anyone can ever do is harm a business owner.

Have you ever....

- Tapped a line of credit or second mortgage so you could give your employees their paycheck?
- Paid off all your vendors and creditors, even though it meant canceling a long-awaited vacation?
- Heard about someone in need and helped them out, even though you knew you would eventually end up borrowing the money – you didn't have it, but you gave anyway because it was the right thing to do?

The entrepreneurs I meet do stuff like that *all the time.* Every time you see a new business or experience a new product for the first time, you can thank an entrepreneur for sticking out his or her neck.

When the unemployment rate drops a measly 0.1%, it's because hundreds of thousands of risk-taking entrepreneurs decided to write a check and hire someone.

And with that in mind....

...When's the last time you turned on CNN and heard an encouraging story about business owners doing good in the world?

When's the last time you heard somebody in the media or education system say, "We need to build up entrepreneurs, because new businesses are the foundation of our communities?"

You're reading this book because YOU are an entrepreneur. And, unfortunately, the world is in a conspiracy to take you out before you get a chance. It's like those nature shows where the predator thinks bird eggs are d-e-l-c-i-o-u-s – especially *just* before they hatch.

Stores, auto repair shops, and restaurants alike get pitched every day with, "I'll get you on the first page of Google." Little do they usually know how slimy many of those pitchmen are.

Truth is, they're worse than incompetent. Thieves preying on thriving businesses. Some of the stories Scott Dennison is about to tell you about these very real threats will raise the hair on the back of your neck.

Well, we can moralize all we want about the parasites that prey on small business owners, but the reality is, you and I have to be smart enough to smoke those people out. We have to see if they can really *prove* what they say is true.

To do that, you have to get a sound direct marketing education.

Here, Scott has provided a concise, fundamental, and elegant road map to the most important parts of generating leads online. After reading this book, your chances of getting duped instantly drop 90%. You'll know how to hire consultants, experts, and services…because you're miles farther in doing these things for yourself.

Nobody will be able to pull the wool over your eyes when you understand the success criteria better than the salesmen do.

And…once you've survived that gauntlet, you'll find the herd is thin. The ones left standing – well, they certainly have the smell of battle on 'em.

You'll find that, contrary to stereotypes, entrepreneurs are actually EXTREMELY generous. Heck, they're just so happy to be sitting across the table eating burgers with someone who UNDERSTANDS them, they'll tell you anything you wanna' know. Every syllable drips with experience and struggle and victory.

The entrepreneurial life is one where you fail more often than you succeed. You come to understand there is something blessed, maybe even sacred, about failure.

The struggle has this odd way of letting you know your place in the world. As long as you don't get complacent, it keeps your ego solidly in check.

You know that half the things you think are true probably aren't, and half the things you KNOW are true are almost certain to change next week.

You surf the edge of chaos, enjoying the thrill of the ride. The agony and the ecstasy.

Some people said you'd never be anybody. You had ADHD or you were a "C" student, or you couldn't concentrate, or you were a pain in some teacher's butt – or whatever.

They judged you however they judged you.

But, they didn't know YOU. The real you deep inside, the one who decided, somewhere along the way, that dodging the swinging tire irons and rolling with the punches was better than a life of quiet desperation.

And now, with Scott's help, you can also generate a lot more leads and grow your business a LOT bigger.

Seize the Day.

—**Perry Marshall, March, 2015**

Introduction

If you're over age 35 and you haven't spent years living in a cave or something, you probably know who Anthony Robbins is. He's that tall, dark, motivational speaker who, for much of the 1990's, was on television somewhere in the US, almost literally 24 hours per day, 7 days per week, selling his immensely popular *Personal Power* program.

He's still at it today – *just not quite everywhere, like before.*

What you probably *don't* know is that ol' Tony and I are related – which is different from saying we're *relatives* – but, we *are* indeed related.

Here's how:

We both had the same mentor (the late Jim Rohn) and we both held the same job in the same company – just 20 years apart: we both spent (invested) a period of our lives working to help regular people connect with Mr. Rohn's unique and powerful message.

Here's why:

One of the most profound and important things Mr. Rohn ever told me while I was working for him was that it didn't matter where I was starting from – just that I get started in the direction of my dream.

It does seem that everyone, everywhere, is waiting to get started, waiting to gather the right tools, or to gain more expertise – waiting for *something* to happen or change before taking that big step toward their dreams.

The message here, of course, is that waiting will *never* get you to where you could be if you just get started moving in the right direction.

Mr. Rohn knew this well. That's why a companion lesson of his was, "No matter where you start out – if you study a subject for five years, you can become an expert. If you continue until you've been at it for ten years, you'll become a world-class expert."

True. I'm living proof of this wisdom. This is why, after 20+ years, I believe I've got a pretty good handle on this whole marketing thing.

There are two points I want to make here…

First, if your marketing isn't attracting the ideal customers you want or as many as you need to feel you're succeeding,

you should start heading in that direction. If you continue to work on it – you'll eventually get there.

Second, you may discover, as you get moving in the right direction, that you need some training and mentoring along the way.

You might even decide I could help you.

I wrote this book to help and you're probably reading it right now because you're ready to get moving.

Tony Robbins took the lessons of a great teacher and fashioned a unique life for himself. I studied under the same man and am doing exactly the same thing.

Perhaps *this* is what you need most...

I've worked with a *lot* of small business owners to improve their marketing in the years I've been doing this and there's one thing I learned – because I've heard it over and over again: they want their phone to ring! They *all* want more leads.

I'll bet you do, too. In fact, I'll bet this problem is positioned squarely at the heart of what's currently blocking you from moving forward, if you're not moving toward your goals quickly enough.

For most, the different marketing ideas they've tried haven't yet made their phone ring enough or produced enough leads for them to grow their businesses effectively. Whether it's print ads, billboard ads, Yellow Pages ads, ValPak ads, or any of the other myriad things they've tried – they've all failed to produce the amount of business they want.

There's a simple explanation for this – the Internet.

Recent studies show almost 90% of people now go online looking for the things they plan to buy, or for the services they need. Rarely do we dig out the phone book or flip through the pages of the newspaper. No – we now turn to the Internet first.

Most small business owners already know this. What they don't know, however, is how to make the Internet work for them as it should.

Which leads me to something else I've heard repeatedly, in all those years of discussions with business owners: the Internet is *confusing*.

If you think about it, the confusion is easy to understand. There's SEO (**S**earch **E**ngine **O**ptimization). There's also paid advertising – also known as AdWords (on Google), or pay-per-click (PPC) advertising, which is now available on most search engines and on a growing number of social media sites.

You have Google My Business (or, is it Google +, Google Local, Google Places, or Google Maps now…it's been all of those in a span of about two years). Confusing? You bet…

Then – there's also the whole world of social media itself.

To make things worse, there are far too many people exacerbating the situation with claims that they know how it all works and they can help. These people offer their assistance to small business owners but, all too often, prove they don't really know how to generate leads for their clients at all.

This could easily serve as the checklist of reasons why I wrote this book. At least the start of one. I'm sure I'll go off on some other tangents along the way. Possibly an outright rant or two. Ask any of my clients or the readers of my blog and you'll find that's how I am.

As such, I've also dared myself to accomplish several goals here. First – I want to share with you the biggest mistakes I see small business owners making too often in their marketing and lead generation. Second – I want to discuss both SEO and PPC advertising, to tell you how and when each should be used to maximize your Internet lead generation results.

PPC, in case you didn't know, has the ability to generate leads *within a week*, if not a few hours, of starting a campaign. SEO, on the other hand, takes a while, because you need to get your website set up properly and get it ranking for many of your valuable keywords. For this reason, in many of the campaigns we do for our small business clients, both are used simultaneously.

By following what I'll show you, you will often produce a return on your investment that's many times greater than you're now seeing from any other marketing you could possibly do or ever have done in the past.

Also, I want to show you that your success from doing this is defined as a significant amount of growth in leads coming in that delivers an ROI more than capable of helping you achieve your biggest business goals.

In short – following this plan *will* make your phone ring.

Even better – this can all be mapped out and you can track your results every step of the way, growing your business through the proper application of what is known as the "80-20 Rule."

This rule provides you with a simple, effective way to attain sustainable success. It's so basic, I'm consistently amazed by the screaming absence of its application in business today.

It won't be absent in your business after I'm through with you here.

To clarify, *Wikipedia* defines the 80-20 Rule – also known as the *Pareto Principle* or "The Law of the Vital Few" – this way:

"...for many events, roughly 80% of the effects come from 20% of the causes."

That sums it up pretty succinctly. When you use the Internet to generate business leads the way I'll show you in this book, this rule will provide constant guidance, so you can focus *only* on those efforts that are generating the greatest return.

Once you've started seriously putting the power of this rule into action, you'll find many aspects of life to which it can be applied. In virtually any business, however, the 80-20 Rule most often reveals itself first as, "80% of your sales come from 20% of your clients."

This realization can be a huge eye-opener. It can easily bring about dramatic improvements in sales, marketing, and overall operating efficiency – in a step-by-step way that makes it easy to measure your progress as you go.

If this sounds a lot like the "holy grail" almost every business needs, that's because it pretty much *is*. For this reason, I've chosen the 80/20 rule as the overall unifying focus of this book about Internet marketing.

When our time together comes to an end, you'll see how it can be used to easily map out where you are now, spot what's working for you and what isn't, and make the adjustments necessary to kick your marketing and business growth into the fast lane. In this way, it will act as both measuring stick and compass.

This isn't a book *about* the 80-20 Rule itself. But, it plays such a vital role in virtually everything I do for my clients that it's deeply ingrained in every aspect of the Internet marketing tactics I'll be laying out for you here.

Some changes will be required...

The 80-20 Rule, sadly, can't be applied effectively to the outdated marketing you've most likely been doing in the past. Unfortunately, it makes determination of a clear-cut ROI difficult to track.

To follow along and realize the changes you were hoping to find here, you'll need to change the way you do your marketing from this point forward.

Don't worry. I promise to keep the transition as painless as possible for you.

Finally, I also feel the need to guide you around some of the pitfalls you'll surely run into, if you haven't already. I wish it wasn't necessary, but there are so many so-called "SEO and Internet Marketing Experts" currently flooding Main Street USA with disinformation and downright incompetence it's my hope I can guide you around them here, so you don't bring in the wrong outside help as you build your business with online leads.

Actually, helping you avoid falling into the traps these people are so adept at planting has become something of a mission of mine.

Lower casualties helps win the war...

If you sat where I do, meeting with so many business owners, you'd see the problem more fully.

Too often, entrepreneurs become the casualties of these schemes that often leave them much worse off than when they started.

Many of these schemes are intended to take advantage of those who buy into them, sadly, at a time when the buyer needs more help than ever to succeed.

Instead, they weaken them by draining away their marketing budgets with little or nothing in return, damaging our overall economy in the process.

I fight against that almost every day.

If you follow my blog and newsletters at all, you'll see I've been engaged in the battle to educate business leaders like yourself against these schemes for a long time now. I *want* to see businesses prosper, not wither and die from bad marketing or endless expenses that simply can't provide a reasonable ROI.

This is not totally altruistic on my part. I've also found I make a lot more money doing what I do to help my clients when they prosper and thrive as a result of what I do for them. Apparently, the schemers and scammers of Main Street don't "get" this aspect of doing business. They might operate differently if they could see that actually *helping* business owners with services that matter is more profitable, in the long run, than simply taking them for whatever they can get and moving to the next victim.

First, of course, they'd have to actually know what's needed to help the businesses they're victimizing with their schemes.

If you've ever fallen victim to one of these less-than-savory people, don't feel badly. You probably assumed they had souls. You most likely thought they'd have the same attitude about their businesses and serving their clients as you and I do.

Don't. Assume. Anything.

Make no mistake about it – I'm not just "trying to be a salesman" here. I don't have to be. My ideal client *wants* what I'm offering. They *want* to dominate their market. They see it as their *right* to capture as many sales as possible – and I agree. They also feel it's their *duty* – to their employees, to their employees' families, and to their own families – to grow their businesses to their full potential in sales and profits and I love nothing more than helping them do so.

This goal, however, can *only* be achieved with exceptional marketing. I don't care how cool or new or exciting your particular mouse trap is, you'll never actually sell the number of them you deserve to sell without exceptional marketing to help make that happen.

I don't care how COOl or new or EXCITING your particular mouse trap is, you'll NEVER actually SELL the number of them YOU DESERVE to sell --

WITHOUT EXCEPTIONAL MARKETING to... HELP MAKE IT HAPPEN.

~ Scott A. Dennison

That's what my clients have come to expect from my team. I'm not asking you to believe me simply because I *said* it. Instead, I intend to *show* you – via this book.

Welcome aboard the Internet lead generation train. Clients and friends often call me *"The Marketing Geek"* and I'll be your guide on the journey. We're ready to pull out of the station and it's good to have you on board.

I'll do my best to keep the ride interesting for you.

—Scott A. Dennison

CHAPTER
ONE

Would You Like a Slurpee™ with that SEO?

In this chapter, you will learn:

- Why your current marketing will most likely fail...

- How the Internet can turn things around!

- Know when you need outside help

- How to avoid the lying lairs lurking along the path

In almost every conversation I have with business leaders, they tell me what they want most from their advertising and marketing is to make the phone ring more often – to get calls from prospects interested in the products and services that they're selling.

Like it or not, effective optimization (SEO) and the visibility in search engines that results is the backbone of online business lead generation today. Being found at the top of search engine results is what it takes today to make your phone ring more often.

There's actually more to it, and I'll get to all that in just a bit. First, virtually every week, I'm asked by clients and readers about my thoughts on the best SEO service[1] options available. After all – SEO can be a bit tricky. There are several important moving parts you have to get lined up the right way, to get it all working correctly. It's natural to seek some outside help when getting this part of your online lead generation marketing set up.

When they ask, people quickly learn I *do* have an opinion about it – more likely a rant. Or two.

That's because there are a lot of crazy scams and posers running around claiming to be SEO "experts" and it often confuses the issue.

I have to admit, I've had just about enough of the endless parade of scammers and spammers who send emails to businesses – including me – trying to say they're the best SEO service on earth.

It's gotten so bad I halfway expect, whenever talking with some of these people, to hear them ask if I'd like a Slurpee™, to complete my order. I'm often tempted to ask for one. At least then I'd get *something* in return for my money.

How about you?

I think it's best, before I start lining out some best practices for you to follow, if we first look at this scourge on our planet and go over what you definitely need to avoid. You can't make progress moving forward if you're kicked backward

---

[1] http://scottadennison.com/seo-optimization-tips-tutorial/

down the path by the kind of "help" any of these people tend to offer.

Here's an example:

A few months ago, I received an email from a guy who told me he's the only "pay for performance" SEO firm ever created. His pitch? According to him, this is absolutely the *best* way to buy SEO services because, if it doesn't work, you don't pay.

That's *not* what this guy's terms of service said – but I'll come back to that in just a bit.

It *does* sound good. Unfortunately, even if the deal was *exactly* as presented, there are lots of red flags flying on this offer – and I see them often enough to warrant addressing them here and now. If such an offer comes your way, I want you to know how to avoid it.

First – I visited this guy's site and noticed that, for credibility, he's displaying a *"Google Certified"* emblem. I'm very familiar with that program. I know that, when you meet the qualifications for inclusion, Google actually gives you a button that's linked in such a way that, if you click on it, you can verify whether a company really *is* certified by Google as meeting those qualifications.

In this case, the button was just a graphic. It wasn't connected to *anything*. When I clicked on it, nothing happened – because it was a *scam*.

That might explain – at least in part – why most of the portfolio of sites this guy had supposedly worked on weren't in business anymore. To make matters worse, the SEO on his *own* site appeared to have been done by someone who's never done it before.

But wait – it gets *better*.

The domain this site was on was owned by a firm in India, but they're advertising with a U.S. address. I typed the U.S. address into Google Maps and it showed me that this business was apparently operating in a *gas station*, in San Jose, CA!

Maybe he's just a part-timer who works at a gas station…but I doubt it, seriously.

Adding insult to injury, this guy's terms of service indicate that his so-called "pay-for-performance" program costs $2000 per month but, if they don't get results, they'll keep working for *free* until they do. There's nothing wrong with this guarantee, as it stands…unless, of course, the guy offering it is a scammer who doesn't intend to help you beyond your initial $2000 payment anyway.

Unfortunately, if you counted on him to perform, I think you'd be more likely to join the company of those other poor souls listed on this guy's site – with websites banned by Google or out of business altogether – before you ever saw the "results" he claimed he could get.

FRAUDS
pretending to know SEO
are far more common
than you might ever
imagine.

~ Scott A. Dennison

Frauds pretending to know SEO are far more common than you might ever imagine. It's gotten bad enough I always caution the entrepreneurial business leaders I serve to be *very* careful when they're approached with similar offers.

Remember: Internet lead generation – especially SEO – is still a rapidly changing, growing field. Actual certifications and qualifications to provide these services are few. The best certification you can ask for is to look at the results anyone approaching you as a provider has created for *their* clients.

Another, more recent example:

I was approached not long ago by someone on LinkedIn who wanted to connect. My process for approving requests for people I don't know is simple: I look at their profile and see who they are.

You probably do this, too – right?

So, I took a look at this guy's profile. He presents himself as a professional web developer and SEO expert. OK – I'm connected with a number of them now. Some of them are really good at their craft and well worth following. They enable me to keep up with what they're doing and, occasionally, we exchange ideas.

I also saw a link to this guy's website in his information so, off I went to have a look.

Uh-oh!

His site was so bad that, if they were publishing an updated edition of *Web Pages That Suck*[2], his homepage would be on the *cover*. There were no mentions of past clients or links to sites in a portfolio – also a troubling sign. So – instead, I looked at the SEO he'd done on his *own* site…another way to see if someone knows what they're doing when it comes to this type of service.

Again…*uh-oh!*

Still, he's out there trying to convince small business owners to consider him one of best SEO service companies and *pay* him to help them.

Lying Liars Who Pour Out Lies

I warned you I can rail on this aspect of the lead generation business to the point of ranting. I've had too many conversations with business owners who have been lied to just to make a sale.

It can create *real* problems for you going forward and I've had enough of it.

Here's what I'm talking about:

---

[2] http://www.webpagesthatsuck.com/

In one case, a builder hired someone to build them a website in early December. 12+ weeks later, he had nothing to show for his investment and the guy doing the work came back looking for *more* money, claiming he also needed more time to finish the project.

By comparison, my team and I finished a beautiful and powerful lead generation site in about three weeks and it was already ranking for important keywords in Google search results to generate leads for the client.

No need for shame – I've been taken, too…

Yes – problems like this are *so* prevalent that even *I* can still get taken now and then. A few months ago, I hired a programmer to make some changes to the code on my site. An hour or two into his work, I noticed certain elements of my site had disappeared.

Within another hour, *all* the information contained in the sidebars of my site was gone. The site's header graphic was missing, too.

I asked the programmer what was happening. He said, "Oh, yes – don't worry. I'm changing the info from within the database."

Shortly after that, all the site's custom style sheets disappeared. When I started to get upset with him, he disappeared, too. I had to enlist the help of my hosting company to reload a prior version of my site, to correct all the damage one supposedly expert programmer did in just a couple of hours.

Without knowledge, everyone's vulnerable...

You'd think scammers might hesitate to rip off attorneys...right? I met with a local attorney recently who had her firm's domain name *stolen* by a so-called local marketing "expert." Not only had this "expert" transferred the firm's domain name into his own name – he also registered it for *10 years* when he did!

It seems his plan, to ensure that he "gets paid," was to sell the law firm's property *back* to them – or, possibly, to "*rent*" it back to them at a premium – for years to come.

Don't.

Let.

This.

Happen.

To.

You!

The domain name you've registered with which to market your business online is an *asset* of your business. It should appear on the balance sheet in your accounting as such.

> YOUR domain name is an asset of your business.
>
> It should appear on the balance sheet in your accounting.
>
> – Scott A. Dennison

If you doubt that a single domain name could ever really be worth all that much, don't. A quick search for *"most expensive domains"* shows that some are worth millions of dollars.

A little bit closer to home, one client of mine registered his domain about 14 years ago. He was recently offered $350k for that domain.

Are *all* domain names that valuable?

No.

But, your URL has *value*. Treat it that way.

Don't allow (by error, omission, or otherwise) *anyone* to get access to your domain name and transfer it or change ownership of it in *any* way.

Long-distance SEO

You might also get emails from firms all over the world, asking if you want to hire them to *"get you on the first page of Google."*

I know *I* get them.

Here's the thing: millions of pieces of this kind of SPAM are sent out every day by these firms. Most don't even operate in the U.S. *All* of them ignore a core principle of business today: that people do business with people we know, like, and trust.

First and foremost, I'm a passionate advocate for *never hiring a foreign firm to do mission-critical work like SEO*. Why? Because, if something goes wrong, they'll simply disappear and leave you to figure out what happened.

You want to hire the best person you can who understands your industry and your specialty within that industry. For this reason, it's always best to work with someone who is easy to understand and, if at all possible, who works similar hours to yours. This is usually difficult when you work with someone who is located in another country.

Also, when you hire someone to do SEO work on your site, keep in mind they'll need to have administrative rights over your website. This gives them enough power to wreak serious havoc on your business – inadvertently or otherwise. I'm not suggesting this happens regularly but, if that access isn't secured, it could fall into the wrong hands.

If, for example, the passwords and other login details to your website aren't updated or deleted at the end of the project, *your worker – or one of his or her associates – could easily re-enter and hack your site.*

In mere minutes, your entire investment in your website could be gone. This is where that whole "know, like, and trust" thing *seriously* comes into play. In *reverse*. For *you*.

When it comes to hiring someone to help you improve the marketing you're doing online, you want to first fully vet the company you're considering, *before* you hire them. The number one way to evaluate the work they'll do for you is to look at the last six projects they've done for other clients and speak to the people they worked for.

All I can do is sound the alarm for you and hope you heed my warnings. There are lying liars everywhere and you *must* protect yourself. Your marketing budget and the future of your business depend on it.

Finally, don't be one of *these* guys…

One of the best possible ways I know of to avoid being scammed by all the posers out there is to be reasonable in your expectations and understand that you generally get what you pay for.

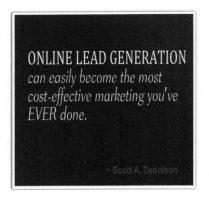

Online lead generation can easily become your most powerful marketing vehicle – the most cost-effective marketing you've ever done. When you *do* find and vet someone capable of handling the task for you, the last thing you want to do is chase them away by signaling with your offer that you doubt their capabilities.

Here's what I mean:

If you've done your due diligence, you should at least know the people you're talking to are qualified professionals with a track record of delivering what they promise. Still, I've talked to far too many business leaders (and, sometimes, their sales teams) who insist that, if I can get them more/better customers *now*, they'll be happy to invest some money in their marketing with me…*later*.

Basically, they're asking me to work free and "earn my keep" by "proving my worth" before I can expect payment.

Look at it this way: If it's cold both outside and inside, there's only one of two possible actions you should take, if you want to improve your conditions: (1) gather some wood and start a fire or (2) walk over to the thermostat and turn the heater on.

It makes no sense to wish for heat when the furnace is off or there's no fire burning in the fireplace. Right?

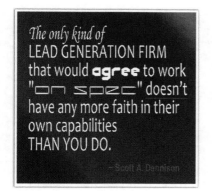

The only kind of LEAD GENERATION FIRM that would **agree** to work "on spec" doesn't have any more faith in their own capabilities THAN YOU DO.

— Scott A. Dennison

What if someone suggested they'll turn up the thermostat or put more wood on the fire for you – *after* there's some heat in the house?

You'd have to laugh, right?

If you think about it, the only kind of lead generation firm that would agree to similar terms doesn't have any more faith in their own capabilities than you've signaled that you do.

You deserve better.

The Results You Seek are There to be Had

The good news is, if you're happy with your marketing and the results you're seeing, fine. If you don't believe what I've written for you in this book will help you, that's ok, too. You can also choose to do the *opposite* of what I tell you. You could hire all the unqualified, unproven outside help you want. You don't *have* to do *anything*.

You most likely turned to this book, however, because you *don't* want things to stay the way they are. Something told you the answers you're seeking just might be in these pages.

Am I right?

If you're in on the side of improving, of getting and keeping more "ideal" customers and/or clients (as I know I am – *all* the time), then I'd like to kick things off by sharing a short exercise for you. You can do it with a calculator and piece of paper, or you can do it with an Excel spreadsheet.

First, you need to dig out the total number of clients you had at the beginning of this year.

Now, look back and determine how many you had at the beginning of last year. Is this year's number bigger than last year?

If you answered, "Yes," – congrats!

Some of you will find you have less this year than last year. That's obviously *not* so good.

We can do the same thing with total revenue. If your revenue is growing, especially at a time when a large number of Americans think the economy is in a recession; you should pat yourself on the back.

If it isn't, now you know it and you can make the decision to change course. My mission, should you choose to stick with me to the final pages, is to make that course clear and hand you the ability to track your results every step of the way to your ultimate goal.

I'm pretty sure, if you apply what I show you in this book, you'll find it was time well spent.

This chapter, I've uncovered some of the slimy "deals" you can expect to find scattered among the gems when you start looking for help with your online lead generation. I also briefly discussed the power of the Internet to provide a solution – possibly the reason why you chose this book to help you – if you're unhappy with the results you're seeing from your current marketing efforts. This paves the way to showing you "how it's done," in the chapters ahead.

CHAPTER TWO

Internet Business Lead Generation is a *Lot* More than SEO

> **In this chapter, you will learn:**
>
> - Why the economy – and other excuses DON'T matter
> - The power of a reliable, repeatable sales system
> - How branding can be a trap
> - How direct, trackable response makes ROI happen
> - The pieces to put in place
> - The secret of the three M's
> - Making PPC pay

Many years ago, motivational speaker and sales trainer, Zig Ziglar, said, "Timid salespeople have skinny kids."

This forces me to ask you a question: How skinny are *your* kids?

I'm not talking about thin children who are at their natural weight. I'm not talking about children who are underweight from dealing with illness, either.

I'm talking about *skinny*. As in, they don't get enough to eat.

If things have been running a bit tighter than you'd like in your business, I have news for you. It's *not* the economy!

Yes. The economy's seen some monumental shifts these past few years. As of this writing, we can turn on the TV, listen to the radio, or pick up any number of newspapers and hear the economy's been struggling. Whether we're still in recession or not, as of this writing, is now widely disputed. Many people think we are – economists say we're not.

It honestly doesn't matter.

Adopting the economy as an excuse for why your business is struggling is a choice *you* make. It has nothing to do with what's going on in the DOW, or in the S&P 500, or in the GDP.

The fact is, whether you might choose to think of it as "bad" *or* "good," the condition of the economy is *never* the reason your business isn't living up to your expectations.

In 2012, for example – when

people were seriously unsure of the financial future of the world – the U.S. economy was still almost 16 *trillion* dollars.

That's trillion – with a *"T."*

Every one of those digits represents a dollar that someone spent. And it's grown since then. That means – whether *your* business is growing or not – *some* people out there are still getting *PAID*. Regardless.

Here's the problem: If you don't have a reliable selling system in place that you operate over and over, then the best you can ever do is hope someone shows up today looking to buy something that you sell.

If hope is your best strategy for capturing and growing more business, chances are your kids *are* skinny. Or they will be, soon enough.

Sorry if that's a little blunt.

We opened our discussion in the first chapter talking about the outrageous stuff you need to avoid, so you hang onto and get the best ROI for the marketing dollars you do choose to spend. Now we need to delve into what you *should* be doing – with an emphasis on *why*.

You've got to use marketing you can reliably TRACK, so you can FOCUS in on what's working best and ELIMINATE what isn't.

~ Scott A. Dennison

To have success in any business – to avoid having skinny kids – you need to identify who your ideal client is, develop a message they'll respond to, and use a form of media to which that ideal client pays the most attention to reach them.

Then, you can simply wash, rinse, and repeat – with one minor twist: Over time, you'll identify the top 20% of your campaigns, so you can keep using them more often. You'll also identify the top 20% of your customers, so you can repeat what you did to find them, to find more just like them.

That means you've also got to use marketing you can reliably track, so you can focus in on what's working best and eliminate what isn't, constantly improving your ROI as you go.

Marketing should *never* be an expense…

Anyone who ever told you marketing is an expense that must be paid – like the utilities or the stockroom staff payroll – was wrong. Marketing – *all* marketing – is an *investment* that deserves a reasonable ROI.

You wouldn't knowingly add a product or service to your business that returned less than it cost you to provide. Still, countless businesses do this, day in and day out, when it comes to the marketing they do to bring in new business.

Don't feel bad. This sort of wrong-headed thinking was prevalent long before there was an Internet. It's what led John

Wanamaker, considered a "pioneer in marketing" by many people of his era, to coin the oft-repeated phrase, "Half the money I spend on advertising is wasted; the trouble is, I don't know which half." This kind of thinking has also led literally thousands of businesses to spend more than they had to trying to build a brand – when they *should* have been focused on attracting more paying clients.

Branding is the form of marketing that drives advertising agencies like the ones you've seen on TV…from *Bewitched* to *Mad Men*…precisely because it *is* so expensive and unpredictable. This is because the results, by and large, are essentially untrackable. These agencies make their money as a percentage of what they can convince their clients they should spend running the ads the agencies create. The branding approach makes total sense…for *the agencies*.

For this reason, after studying every form of marketing there is for a *lot* of years, I've concluded that "branding" is almost always a nearly *complete* waste of time and money for most businesses today.

The branding approach to marketing your business makes total sense…

for the agencies.

If you're doing it, you should stop. Now.

Getting directly to the point…

Consider direct response advertising, instead. With direct response, you're investing in the acquisition of *ideal* clients and customers.

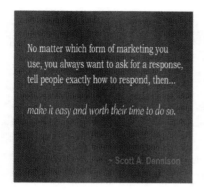

No matter which form of marketing you use, you always want to ask for a response, tell people exactly how to respond, then...

make it easy and worth their time to do so.

~ Scott A. Dennison

With direct response marketing, you're not at all concerned about the nebulous activity known as "branding your business." Instead, you're either going for qualified leads or a low-cost direct sale from everything you do.

When it comes to generating small business leads online, direct response marketing makes it happen. It's what everything I do for my clients is all about – online or offline.

Regardless of which form of marketing you use, you *always* want to ask for a response, tell people *exactly* how to respond, then make it easy and worth their time to do so. When your request is clear, they'll do what you've asked a reliable, measurable percentage of the time.

Direct Response
EQUALS
Measurable Response

~ Scott A. Dennison

Direct response = *measurable* response.

Like I said – as with any investment, you can and *should* expect a return on your investment. The 80-20 Rule can easily be applied to your direct marketing efforts, to help you achieve that return, once and for all, because you'll be able to easily see the results of everything you do quickly enough to make necessary changes that keep you on the track to greater profits – much faster than any other method I know of.

In short, you'll be able to maximize the profitable return you deserve from your marketing dollars. *Predictably.*

Digging in…

I always pay careful attention to what's going on in the world of SEO. You can probably tell, from the way I opened our discussion in this book, that I'm particularly tuned in to the nonsense a lot of so-called SEO "experts" are trying to sell to my clients.

Probably the most annoying of these schemes, as far as I'm concerned, are the ones who come in guns blazing, claiming they'll get you on page one of Google. You'd think this is some kind of Holy Grail of SEO, guaranteed to net you a huge return for your money, to hear them tell it.

While being at the top position of Google for the right keywords can certainly bring you some business, I hope you haven't fallen for this nonsense pitch.

There are a lot of businesses today who "own" the number one spot on Google for a *lot* of keywords – but most still aren't seeing the kind of increase in their business and sales they should for the effort. Far from it.

The process you need to follow is a little more complex than simply occupying a certain position on a Google search page. When you follow the right steps, applying the 80-20 Rule to help clarify and quantify your best approach, however, you'll see the results you were hoping for almost without fail.

Internet business lead generation –it's a lot more than SEO

– Scott A. Dennison

As I said earlier, SEO *is* an integral part of Internet business lead generation – of making your phone ring more often – but there are several related steps involved, to get it right.

Here are the pieces you'll need to put into play, to benefit from an effective online lead generation campaign:

- Clarity on who your ideal client is
- Your business USP (**U**nique **S**elling **P**roposition)
- A process for effective keyword generation/targeting
- Professional landing pages for PPC lead generation
- A well-designed website, built for lead conversion/generation
- Great content, properly optimized for search (one part of SEO)
- Professional back-link campaigns (the other part of SEO)

We'll go through each of these steps in more detail throughout the rest of this book. First, it's important that you understand the marketing principles behind each of these steps.

Free your mind – and increased sales will follow...

Hopefully, you've cleared your head of the notion that all forms of marketing and advertising are good, because they "get your name out there." There are many forms of advertising and marketing to choose from today, but only a few of them will actually generate the response you want and need, making it worth the money you're investing in them.

Whatever advertising you choose to invest in must, for example, be able to generate leads or customers. The ROI must also be in line with other measurable and effective forms of marketing/advertising – or *don't write the check!*

This is similar to how people make other investments. For about a year and a half, in my early 30's, I worked on a team raising money for small businesses. I thought what we had was such an outstanding opportunity I couldn't understand when people said "no" to it. In hindsight, I learned that our investment opportunity was being compared to every other opportunity they had in which to invest the same dollars – including the decision to do nothing at all.

When it comes to marketing your business, your decision process begins when you know who your ideal client or customer is and what their lifetime value is to your business. Then, measure every form of advertising you're doing or plan to do against the job it's doing attracting those customers and apply the 80/20 Rule to those results.

Will it produce the results you need or won't it?

The 80-20 rule dictates that 20 percent of your efforts will produce about 80 percent of the results you're looking for. Likewise, it dictates that 20 percent of your clients (the result of your marketing) will generally produce 80 percent of your total sales. When you're able to continually measure what you're doing and how much you're spending versus the number of leads and/or sales you're generating as a result, you're able to then shift your efforts for maximum effectiveness as you go. Your business is assuredly going to grow in the process.

Do this right and business growth is practically unavoidable.

A website alone is *just* that...

...IN CYBERSPACE, NO ONE CAN HEAR YOU SCREAM

~ Scott A. Dennison

You bought a spot in cyberspace. Where *is* that, anyway? It's a fact that, in cyberspace, no one can hear you scream. Don't for a moment think merely having a website will bring you a lot of business. That might have been true in 1995...for a while. As you probably know...it's grown a *lot* since then. In January, 2014, Google reported that there were about 180 million websites online – at that time. When you think about the size of the Internet and the number of sites online today, it's a bit loony thinking anyone could find your site among all the others now online, without a little help.

Today, there are two basic ways people will find you on the Internet. The first is because someone already has the address to your website. Usually, someone who has your web address or URL already knows you. They're either an existing customer or they might have gotten your business card, or a brochure, or flyer somewhere.

The second way people find you on the Internet is through search engines or, perhaps, through social media. If they *do* find you this way, however, they aren't necessarily looking specifically for you – they're usually looking for something that solves a problem they're having and they do this by typing in words related to the problem.

These people are typically ready to make a buying decision and you want them to find *you* when they type in these keywords – not someone else.

After you've determined precisely what keywords apply best to what you have to offer, here's what you need, to make that visitor decide to buy from you:

1. The information on your web pages must be set up properly and optimized for search.
2. Other, more important sites must link to your site.

There's still more to it – but, when you get just these two elements right, you can get preferred placement in the search engines for important keywords related to your business. If a lot of people are searching for your products and services and you're optimized for search engines on the keywords they're using, you can get visitors coming to your site in growing numbers.

If your website is properly optimized for users, so they can easily make a small "introductory" purchase, or opt-in to your email list – or take some other important next step that leads to more sales for your business – you can do very well.

If your site gets visitors, but they're unsure of what to do, they'll leave and visit a different site. Usually within seconds. Remember how many websites there are on the Internet today? Yeah – they'll go to one of *them*, instead of yours. In a heartbeat. This will increase what is referred to as your site's "bounce" rate.

Believe it or not, Google can and often will penalize you if your bounce rate (the number of people who visit your site from their search results, but "bounce" back away from it quickly) is too high. This can affect your SEO with lower placement of your listing. It can also make your PPC campaigns more expensive, because Google often also charges you a higher per-click rate if your bounce rate is too high.

If your website isn't bringing you the new business and growth you were hoping for, you now know just a few of the reasons why.

Meet the "Three Ms" of marketing...

This key is so powerful, many marketers refer to it as a *"secret."* It's referred to as the "Three Ms."

The Three Ms are:

- **Your market** (your clearly identified ideal client)
- **Your message** (communicating your USP to your ideal client)
- **Your chosen form of media** (the way you communicate that message)

When you have mastery over the market, message, and media, you'll be able to drive action on the part of your ideal clients/customers in increasing numbers.

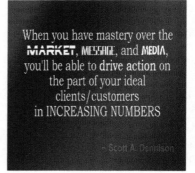

When you have mastery over the **MARKET, MESSAGE, and MEDIA,** you'll be able to **drive action** on the part of your ideal clients/customers in INCREASING NUMBERS

~ Scott A. Dennison

The biggest challenge with the 3Ms for most businesses is often choosing the correct form of media.

Yes, there are dozens, hundreds, maybe even thousands of forms of media available today – but only a few will work in any given situation.

Once you've identified your ideal client (aka: your market)...and you understand all the reasons why people buy the products or services you sell...*and* you've found the best ways to communicate the value of a business relationship with your company (your message)...you just need to focus on determination of the ideal form of media for your campaigns, for maximum success.

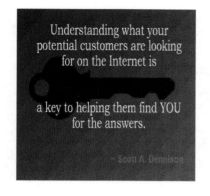
Understanding what your potential customers are looking for on the Internet is

a key to helping them find YOU for the answers.

~ Scott A. Dennison

The truth is, for all of the wonderful things it's made possible, the Internet's still little more than another form of media. As a form of media, the Internet is a wonderfully rich source of information and – because of search engines – it's also reasonably well organized. Certainly more so than almost any other media.

Understanding what your potential customers are looking for on the Internet is key to helping them find you for the answers. It will enable you to place yourself in the path they're following, to the answers they seek.

When you do this, you don't have to be found at the top of the search results for keywords related to the problems you can solve to still get all the business you need.

Account for your conversion rate…

What if you found that, for whatever reason, the traffic you get from search engines converts (opts-in to download something, completes a form, buys something, etc.) at a rate of just under two percent? Then, what if you find out that traffic from sharing information about your good work on your social network converts at a rate of three to four percent?

The social traffic is better, right?

It *can* be – assuming *all* the numbers line up favorably.

In my own case, I invite visitors to my site to opt-in, to receive my regular updates by email. This adds them to a list that I can then reach out to regularly, to continue building a relationship that eventually leads to sales.

Right now, roughly six percent of those who arrive at my site convert by joining that list.

Here's the interesting thing: of those who convert on my site, LinkedIn traffic out-performs search traffic four-to-one. Looking at my opt-ins for just one month, 74% came from LinkedIn traffic and only 18.5% came from search. Roughly 80% from one source.

The 80/20 Rule is a rule for a reason.

If these were your numbers, where would you focus *your* attention?

You'll find out the effectiveness of your marketing by measuring where your traffic's coming from and how many of them are converting in the way you want them to.

What about social media?

Business owners frequently tell me they've heard social media's a great choice for marketing because it's free. Much like SEO, which a lot of people also tend to think is free, social media has a very real cost – either in the time you invest in it or in the size of check you'll write to have someone do it for you.

Some of the costs you can expect include designing a branded look for your social pages and the time needed to research, share content, and engage with people online, to make it work.

Yes – branding still matters – and that's largely what social media is all about. It's just that it should *never* be the end goal of your marketing.

With social media, it's also very important to have your "ear to the ground" in related forums and pages, so you understand what problems, frustrations, or issues prospective customers have that you may be able to solve with your products and services. This can be more time-consuming than you might think. If you're already busy, it's easy to put this task off. This is probably the main reason why most do-it-yourself business social media efforts fail to ever get any traction and generate meaningful leads.

You'll either do your business' social media yourself or you'll hire someone to do the work for you. That's up to you – but always remember your time *is* very valuable.

How you value your time is a matter only you can decide. Usually, it's too valuable for my clients to give up and devote the attention required to properly maintain a social media presence that gets results.

Certainly, if you hire someone skilled in listening on the social networks and doing all the things required to get your business found on the social web, you should expect to pay a reasonable rate for having it done.

Either way – again – meaningful, productive social media work for your business won't be free.

The best form of marketing and advertising for your business will be the one that produces the best overall ROI

Scott A. Dennison

Once again – the best form of marketing and advertising for your business will be the one that produces the best overall ROI. Carefully track your results. Apply the 80-20 rule as you go, to make necessary adjustments to maximize the ROI on your investment, and it won't matter what the actual amount of that investment is.

You will eventually, however, want to ramp up what you spend.

Making pay-per-click pay…

I like pay-per-click (PPC) advertising. A *lot*. It's highly measurable and trackable – and it can provide some of the highest ROI of any type of advertising you'll ever do. However, if you don't do it properly, it can and often does fail to deliver any worthwhile results at all.

The most common mistake businesses make that leads to PPC failure is directing the traffic generated from PPC ads to a generic page, such as the company website's home page.

The person who clicks a PPC ad was looking for something very specific. If they click on your ad – which is when you incur a charge for your advertising (hence the name, pay-per-click) – and they arrive at a page that's not related *specifically* to that ad, they'll hit their "back" button and leave, usually about two-three seconds after they arrived.

Yeah. *That* quick.

The secret to getting exceptional returns on your PPC advertising investment is to use specific "landing pages" that match the information in each of your ads and deliver on the promise you made to get viewers to click in the first place.

If you promise free information about your product or service in your PPC ad – an informative free report, for example – and I click through to your site and find the *same* info on the landing page I see, you have an excellent chance of converting me into a lead.

Nice, huh?

A lot of business owners I talk to are enthralled with PPC advertising. Usually, it's because they've heard stories circulating about businesses who turned a $250 ad budget into tens of thousands of dollars in return. It's the proper use of landing pages in PPC advertising that leads to these reports.

You can find advertising and marketing successes and failures with every type of media that exists today. The best form of advertising for you, however, is the one that produces the highest quantity of ideal clients for your small business at the lowest cost.

In football, winning and losing comes down to the fundamentals: blocking and tackling, as well as running and passing the ball. Winning or losing in business comes down to proficiency in two simple fundamentals: *Getting* and *keeping customers* in a *measurable* way.

If you can measure it, you can make it pay.

When you understand that traffic is traffic and your *real* objective is to get customers who spend money with you, it will all come down to the return on investment you're getting on the different sources of traffic.

> TRAFFIC IS TRAFFIC and YOUR REAL OBJECTIVE is to get customers who spend MONEY with YOU. ~ Scott A. Dennison

You'll only know the ROI when you calculate the lifetime value of the customers you're getting and compare it to what you spent to attract them. Applying the 80-20 Rule to your numbers will help clarify where to place your efforts for maximum ROI.

I decided to write this book about generating online leads because I've found that online leads are returning the best ROI for most of the clients I work with on a daily basis. Some clients get a better ROI on search. Others do better when they focus on social media traffic. Others I work with do very well with pay-per-click traffic. Some do better still with a combination of all of them.

At the end of the day, if you don't know which form of traffic produces the best flow of customers, then all you can do is spend money on marketing and hope for the best.

You'll clearly see by the time you've read this book to the end, that hope is *not* a strategy.

> *I've now revealed to you how, regardless of the current economy or any other outside factors, you can prevent having skinny kids. I've shown you why it's absolutely vital that you identify your ideal clients – and the difference this can make in your life. I also pointed out that there's more to online lead generation than just SEO and I revealed the irreplaceable "Three Ms" you need to apply for lead generation success. Finally, I explained why your marketing isn't an expense…it's an investment…and briefly introduced you to the best way you can make the response to all of your marketing trackable, by applying direct response marketing. You're getting the basics under your belt. Let's keep rolling…*

CHAPTER THREE

Nailing Down the Ideal Client

In this chapter, you will learn:
• Avoiding "you'll do" syndrome
• Nailing down the ideal client
• Reading the signs
• Positioning to reach your ideal target
• Sifting the results in your favor

I see a disturbing trend in business. It's the philosophy of "you'll do."

Almost every business owner I know is looking for new customers. In spite of whatever the economy or any number of other factors might be, the need entrepreneurs have to improve their results never changes. Still, their client attraction process is rarely as tight as it could or should be.

As a result, someone calls, clicks, or otherwise inquires about our products and services and all we really care to know is if they have the ability to pay.

If their answer is "Yes," we tend to reply, "You'll do."

When that happens, we should never be surprised a short time later, when this new customer starts asking about our pricing. Or about our terms. They point to others in our industry and say, "They offer *the same thing* for less than you."

Or, "They do *this, and this, and this* – for the same money. Will you/do you do those, too?"

Now you've got yourself a low-margin, high-maintenance PITA client. That's an acronym. If you don't know what it means or can't figure it out…drop me a note. I'm trying to keep this book "family friendly."

But, this isn't the only area where "you'll do" causes problems.

It works in reverse, too.

Many business owners looking for help will find themselves at, let's say, a networking event where they meet someone who offers this or that service.

Let's use Internet marketing or social media marketing, for example. The conversation goes like this:

You: "What do you do?"

Them: "I do Internet marketing and social media marketing for small businesses."

You: "Really? I've been thinking about doing some of that."

Them: "I can get you on the first page of Google and get you lots of new 'fans' for your Facebook page."

You: "Really? How much is your service?"

Them: "Oh, we're very affordable. Only $XX per month."

You: "You'll do…"

Not exactly a scientific approach to finding the best service provider for your needs, is it?

If you're interested in the long-term health and viability of your business; if you're working to fulfill your "ultimate outcome," you *must* have a client attraction process that's focused on ideal clients…not new fans or page one of Google.

There aren't as many of these ideal clients as there are of the "you'll do" variety. Remember – 20% of your clients produce 80% of your results, but those 20% are also more profitable, lower-maintenance and, working only with them, you'll also find you have a better quality of life.

The same goes for the service providers *you* choose – especially in the online marketing world. Today, it seems if you play on Facebook or Twitter for a few hours a day, you can market yourself as a "social media expert."

Many do.

Likewise, if you read a book or attend a Webinar or two on SEO, you can now market yourself as an "SEO expert."

Many do this, too.

But, if you want your site to be a useful tool, one that generates leads and helps you grow your sales to those type of customers you *really* want most, you need to choose who you work with to get the work done wisely.

You need to make a choice based on ROI – *not* on cost.

You simply *must* identify your ideal clients. It's the only way you can reliably focus your marketing efforts to find your ideal customers where they reside.

It's so important, I've only just begun hammering you on the forehead with reminders.

Allow me to continue hammering home the point:

She threw my sample like a discus!

Have you ever been out on a sales call and come across someone who could be described as "mercurial?" Perhaps "nearly bi-polar" would be a more accurate description.

I remember the day well. I was a rep for an outdoor electric sign company at the time. We made our living doing some of the most difficult kind of cold call selling possible. The easiest way to describe it was that I would drive around, looking at the signs in front of businesses. If I drove past your business and decided your sign was weak or ineffective, I'd stop in to talk to you about it.

One out of every three business owners who agreed to have that discussion with me would end up ordering a new sign from me within two hours.

A sale of two grand or more from one out of three. Nice!

Unfortunately, this *one* day didn't quite work out that way.

I walked in like I would on any other occasion. I met the owner and, using my well-practiced opening, she agreed to take a look at a sample of what we were offering.

I went out to the car and grabbed my sign sample, along with some other presentation materials, and went back in.

So far, so good. I was on my way to my one of three.

My presentation always started with a discussion of how effective a good sign can be – especially on a busy highway like the one this lady's business was on. Then, I'd talk about their average sale and what a customer was worth.

If it all went well, I'd then begin to develop a concept of what a new sign for them would look like.

Somewhere early in the discussion, however, this lady decided she'd heard enough. Unfortunately, I wasn't going to give up so easily – so I continued with my show-and-tell routine.

About a minute later, she ripped the plug from the wall, grabbed my sign sample from the counter, and threw it like a discus toward the door – about 20 feet away.

It landed on the floor with a great crash.

It was obvious the light bulbs inside the sign were all broken. Still, I half expected her to rush over and kick or stomp on it some more, just to make certain it was really broken.

Thankfully, she didn't.

I told you this story so you could benefit from what I learned by experiencing it:

Some people and businesses make ideal clients – and some don't. Truthfully, in the case I just related to you, I was trying to make a square peg fit into a round hole. I was pushing a bit to make that happen when she "went off."

Prospects give off clues with their body language. It's been said that 90+% of communication is non-verbal, but I ignored the clues and made my goal more important than hers. She sensed that and forcefully shut the conversation down.

Sorting out your prospects FIRST is BETTER, EASIER, and MORE EFFECTIVE than trying to sell EVERYONE

~ Scott A. Dennison

Sorting out your prospects first is better, easier, and more effective than trying to sell *everyone*. There are some who are interested in what you're offering. Others won't be. It's possible that, while you're trying to sell to the one who isn't interested, you're missing an opportunity to sell to someone who is.

Imagine the impact it would have on your life if your business served *only* ideal clients/customers on an almost exclusive basis. Do they understand that your business – like every other – needs to be able to provide value while still making a profit? Or, are they more inclined to grind you for every last nickel in the deal?

Minute by minute...

If you're stuck working with anyone and everyone who responds to your marketing (or lack of marketing, in many cases), instead of working with those who are your ideal customers, you'll find yourself stuck with more clients like the one who wrote me this email the other day:

"I'm asking that you refund one half of the (fee) because, in my opinion, you have not performed per the promises made during our phone conversations. The remaining (fee) is ample compensation for the (work completed)."

Her note reminds me of a joke (you didn't see that coming, did you?)...

A dentist tells a man needing a tooth extraction that the fee will be $125. The guy's primary question was, "How long will it take?"

The doc tells him it'll take two minutes.

The man then yells, "$125 – for *two minutes* of work?"

The doc then calmly replies, "Once I grab your tooth with my pliers, we can take as long as you'd like for me to pull it."

Besides wondering where I find some of these jokes, you might be asking, "What's this got to do with our discussion about positioning?"

I mention it because I screwed up in taking this client in the first place. I could have easily passed on the project to begin with – but I didn't.

Most of my ideal clients have a high-priced service that they sell. I've become known for helping them get visibility in their market – usually through SEO – generating lots of leads for them to sell to. Doing this consistently makes my fee irrelevant. If they invest "X" in my services, but get "X-Y-Z" in return, the fee I require for my help is small potatoes to them.

You should seek to position yourself the same way. Then you'll avoid facing the situation I did with that unhappy client.

I chose to work with this particular person, even though her business was already struggling and her average ticket was small. We set out to get some traffic looking at her offers quickly and we moved stuff around on her site, to improve conversion rates. I also recruited an associate who jumped in, again at significantly reduced fees.

Then, I find that she's calculating my value on some standard that's different from my own.

My bad!

Whenever someone tells you they know what *your* adequate level of compensation is, your positioning is off. The idea that I didn't deliver on my promises is nuts – I poured a ton of time and energy into this project. I could easily blame her, if I wanted – but this result was *my* fault. I picked the *wrong client* to pour my time and energy into.

Sifting and sorting…

When you take a slipshod, shotgun approach to your marketing, attracting the most desirable customers is a nearly unattainable goal. With a targeted direct marketing approach, however, the majority of customers you attract to your business can be that ideal customer. You just have to identify the ideal target and fire those arrows at the bulls eye.

That's all very good. But – what if you've already got a list of customers? Are you now left to find out which of them is your ideal, after they've exhibited some of the most undesirable traits to identify themselves?

Maybe not.

If you keep records of your sales and which customers purchased what, there's a process you can follow. If not – you need to start doing so right now.

Here's an exercise for you…

Assemble the information from your records over the past year or two that allows you to see:

- Sales by product/service
- Profits by product/service
- Marketing campaigns/results

Once you've done this, diligently apply the trusty 80-20 Rule to your data. Go line-by-line through the list you just assembled and identify the products or services that – either by revenue or by units of sale – are in the top 20%.

You'll find your list of *best* customers among those buying the top 20% most profitable products or services you sell.

Once you've identified a list of your most profitable customers, go through it again. This time, remove any from the list who you already know, from personal experience, created the biggest problems – or those who consistently nickel-and-dimed you at every step. They might make you money – but it's never worth the effort or aggravation, in the end. Move them over to the "less-than-desirable" list.

The more of this type of data you collect, the more precise you can be here. Worst-case, identify 20% of your most profitable customers. Start from there, if that's all you can do. Then, track the results on all future customers going forward.

Here's where the fun (and maybe some pain, too) comes into the exercise:

For those who are your best, most ideal clients and customers, write down *how you attracted them* to your business.

Ask yourself – *which campaign did they respond to*? If you keep copies of every campaign you've run in the past year or two, get them out so you can review them. This will help you identify your most effective message, when it comes to attracting your ideal customer or client.

Next, turn your attention to the group of less-than-ideal clients/customers. Ask yourself – *which campaign or promotions did* <u>*they*</u> *respond to?*

Stop – or at least *change* – those campaigns or promotions!

If all your customers are glommed together into a single list, with no indication of who buys what – you have a bit more work to do. In this case, you should at least pick out those you know are more trouble than they've been worth.

Next, do some targeted direct marketing to the *rest* of the list, offering something that will appeal only to your ideal customers. This can help you identify some more ideal prospects to work with more often when they raise their hands.

This exercise will give you clarity about many things and help you map out future promotions and offers you can use to build your business.

It won't be long before you find you're *only* working with the best-of-the-best customers, enjoying your work more, and making more money in the process.

Touch your finger to your temple and say, "A-HA! *Now* I understand…"

> *This chapter, I revealed the "you'll do" syndrome we all must battle from time to time, and how to get past it for better marketing results. I showed you some steps you can use to identify ideal clients and, hopefully, to keep less-than-desirable clients away from your door. And – I ran through a*

way you can do this with your existing client base, moving the best of the best to the top, where they can get the focus they deserve. This is the power of knowing your ideal client and applying the 80/20 Rule to find them and sell them more.

Now you're ready to take the next steps.

CHAPTER FOUR

Defining Your USP

In this chapter, you will learn:

- "Voodoo Lounge" USP secrets

- Positioning to increase your profits

- The Soup Nazi approach

- Rendering the competition forgettable

- The burgers and beavers lesson

I assume you're familiar with the legendary rock band, The Who. They have a song with a title that says it all..."Who Are You?"

When I work with clients, helping them indentify their Unique Selling Proposition (USP), that song runs constantly through my head.

Who *are* you? It's what your USP is all about.

Come along with me as I jump into the time machine and tell you a story from the past that's filled with wonder and intrigue...

Rockin' it...

My friend, Ben, was a musician with a dream. He wanted to be a concert engineer, so he put himself on a career path that would lead him to become one of the world's top video engineers.

In that role, he went on to work with the biggest bands on earth – Metallica, Shania Twain, Jimmy Buffett, and Tim McGraw – to name but a few.

In the early 90's, I was a budding entrepreneur who was doing sales jobs by day and searching for the right opportunity nights and weekends.

In February, 1992, a chance meeting in Lakeland, Florida set the stage for the two of us to enter into the secret backstage world of the Rolling Stones Voodoo Lounge, just two years later.

Ben had recently been certified in the newest concert video projectors. He decided he wanted to see if he could leverage this new certification to meet the video crew who, at the time, was touring with U2.

Long story short, we met and built a relationship with the two people who were key players in concert video production. They opened the doors and invited us into the "inner circle" of what goes on backstage.

As Ben's wingman, I got into places most only dream of.

In 1994, the Rolling Stones were in Tampa and that relationship provided us with tickets in the 10th row to see the show, along with backstage passes.

The craziness of the Stone's "voodoo lounge" itself is still burned into my memory.

To think the band traveled with this elaborate backstage environment, setting it up in cities all over the world, is still almost unbelievable.

Before you think there's no possible tie to your business here, read on...

Very few businesses (the Rolling Stones *are* most certainly a business) do *anything* that their customers think about and write about 20 years after the fact.

I was spurred to share this with you because I just had a conversation 20+ years later with a business owner/friend of mine. He truly has the opportunity to position himself, separate and apart from anyone who wants to compete with him – but he just won't do it.

Instead, it's easier for him to sell his products on eBay and complain about the margins provided by the marketing vehicle he's chosen.

PRICE is ONLY a factor... when YOUR PROSPECT can't tell YOU apart from YOUR COMPETITION

~ Scott A. Dennison

You see – people *do* talk about his product in glowing terms. They can't believe the quality of the transmissions he delivers to Jeep enthusiasts, which far exceeds that of others in his industry. But, he persists in thinking that people only buy based on price.

I say, "Bullsnot!"

I've said this before, but price is *only* a factor when your prospect can't tell you apart from your competition. However, if you position yourself in a way that makes it easy to see that you do more and are clearly better – there's a part of your market that will pay almost *any* price to buy from *you* – regardless of price.

This is what developing the right USP is all about.

How about U...2?

Maybe you're not a Stones fan. Even if you are, you might never have been backstage at one of their shows. Ok. Fair enough. Have you ever had the good fortune (in my opinion, anyway) to see a U2 concert in person? Smoke, lasers, lights, music, and the spectacle of the world's biggest band, up-close?

Maybe you've never been able to get a ticket before; maybe you never cared to. If you have, the one thing that's inescapable is that every venue, in every part of the world they choose to play, is always *sold out*.

There's so much demand and so little access that people spend fortunes traveling great distances and even paying enormous scalper prices if the tickets are gone, to go and see it for themselves – just to be able to tell the story.

Ask me. I've been fortunate to have seen them in Miami, Houston, San Diego, Lakeland, Florida and twice in Tampa.

It's ok if you call me a fan-boy. I'll confess to the charge.

But – here's what this has to do with *your* marketing: *Everything* about U2 is positioning – to the maximum.

Positioning, by definition, is about combining authority *and* scarcity together into a volatile mix. People, by nature, want what they feel they can't have and they'll pay high prices to get it. Positioning, by its nature, helps filter out those customers who are not your ideal.

But, too many marketers never think in these terms. They sell products or services that are so widely available as to be considered commodities. By their nature, the only thing people care about with commodities is the price.

But – not *you*.

I'm challenging you – right now – to create some "rattle and hum" around what you do. Position yourself as an authority who can only help so many people at one time.

"Take a number, please – we'll call you when it's your turn."

Scarcity will help separate you from price-peddlers, increase your margins, attract the best-of-the-best clientele, and make your efforts more financially rewarding.

The truth is that U2's music isn't "better." Their show isn't more dazzling than others that I've seen before – or since. But, it's rare to be able to say, "I was there."

That matters to me, and it matters to a lot of other people, too.

When your name comes up, do *your* customers or clients say, proudly: "I get to work with (your name/business name)?"

When you get this part of the equation down pat, the rest of what I have to show you in this book will fall into place much easier.

NO Soup for You!

When I think about the power of establishing a USP for your business, the memory of the Seinfeld *"Soup Nazi"* episode pops into my head.

I assume everyone's seen that show.

One great scene involved a conversation George had with the Soup Nazi, as he moved through the line to get his coveted bowl of soup:

"Um, excuse me, I – I think you forgot my bread."

"Bread, two dollars extra."

"Two dollars? But everyone in front of me got free bread."

"You want bread?"

"Yes, please."

"Three dollars!"

"What!?"

"No soup for you!"

There are so many marketing lessons hidden in that exchange I could hold an entire seminar and not cover them all – but I'll focus on just one right now:

The Soup Nazi had positioned himself brilliantly with his target audience. That positioning had people wanting what he had so badly they almost cowered in fear that he might not sell it to them.

This desire for the product – and the fear they can't have it – provides a business with *all* the leverage.

Fortunately, you don't have to be a "Soup Nazi" to have a similar positioning with your audience. All you really have to do is be so clear in your communication and your USP that everyone who wants or needs your products and services knows that you do business on your own terms.

You want me to lower my price? No soup for you!

You want me, because you didn't plan ahead, to push other customers back in line, so you can reach your deadlines? No soup for you!

I think you get it…

The Seinfeld "Soup Nazi" was a fictional character. But, much of that show was based on real-life experiences of living in

New York. I understand the "Soup Nazi" was based on one such real business.

I'm not saying we want or need our customers to fear us or our business practices. I'm certain the Seinfeld version of the real "Soup Nazi" was a bit exaggerated. I *am* saying, however, that, when you over-deliver, when you consistently out-perform your competitors, when you market yourself properly – prospects will know that it's *you* who will ultimately decide whether or not you want to sell to *them*.

Compare that to those meek and fearful business owners who do business with anyone who shows up. The ones who lower their prices because prospects tell them that their competitors are cheaper. Those who will do more tricks than a trained seal to make an abusive customer happy.

Some businesses will do more tricks than a trained seal to make an abusive customer happy.

DON'T DO IT!

~ Scott A. Dennison

DON'T DO IT!

EVER!

Instead, just tell them – "No soup for you!"

In a world filled with "me-too" businesses, with so many businesses begging for customers and willing to throw themselves – figuratively or otherwise – into a pit of snakes to close a sale...this approach, alone, will turn your unique selling position into a position of real strength and profits.

Your USP and the competition...

Understand that, unless you operate in a vacuum, you have competition. It might not be someone in your area selling *exactly* what you sell. It could just as easily be someone on the Internet or in the next town over.

It could even be another, totally unrelated business that's pulling revenue your ideal customer used to spend with you.

I talked to a retailer of antiques and gifts in Kansas who once told me, "I have over a million dollars in inventory. I own a store filled with things no one *needs*. Everything in here is a discretionary purchase."

His problem? His sales had dropped dramatically ever since a new Indian casino had opened just outside of town and he was convinced there simply wasn't any more discretionary money left to come to him.

I pointed out that most of the casinos in Las Vegas, Atlantic City, and Mississippi are surrounded by high-end shops. Many of them actually rent their space from the casinos, so they can be close by. I also noticed these shops aren't grocery stores or pharmacies. They're luxury items and souvenirs. Things people don't *need*.

They place those shops there because they know *some* people win. When they do, they tend to spend it – often on things they wouldn't ordinarily buy. Even better, the amount those winners spend is usually far and above what they would have otherwise considered plunking down for things they don't need on a day-to-day basis.

Even the casino losers who were smart enough to leave before they went broke leave with discretionary cash they brought to spend. Many wind up spending it in those shops, rather than throwing more good money after bad in the casino.

That antique and gift shop owner changed his positioning, adding the message to his marketing that you should have a treat now and then, because you *deserve* it – and when you buy yourself something nice from his store, it can actually be an *investment*.

He got that message into the media where he knew casino fans were paying attention.

Sales went back *up*. Because his was one of the prime antique retailers in the area, with the most luxurious and expensive collection of goodies for miles around, he started making a *lot* of sales to people who had gone out to the casino and *won*, probably along with some sales to people with money still in hand they decided they'd rather spend elsewhere.

The rest wished they could become a member of that "inner circle" who could buy something there for themselves.

Your USP is that special something that makes your business and what you do for your customers and clients truly different. It should be easy to communicate in your marketing and appeal to the ideal customer or client you're seeking.

It should never, *ever*, be price alone. Instead, you should focus on what it is about you that you uniquely bring to your business. Something special that your business does differently.

Remember Wendy's hamburgers? There were already plenty of choices when it came to buying a burger when they came along. When the late Dave Thomas stepped forward and told the story about naming his restaurants after his daughter…it became something truly different in a sea of sameness – a family-style approach to fast food.

Burger King, with their "have it your way" USP, originally built their restaurants as near to a McDonalds as they could. That message spoke to the people going to that location – people already looking for a hamburger and ready for another choice.

Burger King had no fear of their leading competitor. They knew they'd differentiated themselves enough to benefit by being located as near to their competition as they could be.

Bingo.

Bare your teeth…

I'm sure you've figured out by now that I'm a big fan of great marketing. I applaud those who courageously identify *exactly* who their market is, then go on to create marketing that "speaks their language."

When you do this with your business, in a way that stands out and makes you memorable, you should expect to see outsized growth to your revenue and profits.

Smoke, lasers, and learning to play the guitar aren't required.

Contrary to popular belief – I *do* occasionally need to dress in business attire and go see both prospective and actual clients.

The rumor that I only work in shorts and flip-flops every day has *never* been proven…

When I *do* have the occasion to meet with people outside my home office, I like to wear a good pair of khaki pants. Unfortunately, the brand that I've worn for years – you know, the huge company with a name that starts with an "L" – has (in my opinion, anyway) lowered the quality of its khaki pants. It's gotten to the point where I won't buy them anymore.

Enter Duluth Trading Company. I saw an online ad for their cotton chino pants and decided to give them a try. They use classic "risk reversal" in their marketing by saying if I didn't like them, I could return them for a refund and they would even pay for the return shipping.

Sold.

When the package arrived, written on the outside was the slogan, "Tougher than an angry beaver's teeth."

It's short and sweet, but still transmits a clear message of what the product has to offer. It's very memorable, too. A perfect USP. I *love* it.

The key, here, is developing a USP that's memorable – one that resonates with your target market – then sticking with it.

Twisting in the wind...

Have you ever played Twister? You remember that game, right? It's the party game where you lay out a sheet of plastic with something looking similar to a checker board on it on the floor. Each square on the sheet has a different color dot in it.

Then, you spin the dial and place either a hand or a foot on the appropriate matching color. Soon, all the players are all twisted up around each other and it becomes a game of who can stand the longest – usually in the weirdest of positions – without falling.

There are many parallels between that game and the way many of us do our marketing. Today we're trying to reach for blue, tomorrow for green.

Then, we get twisted up in a mess and fall down.

The problem with this is that your ideal client can't keep up with the changes, so they simply do business somewhere else.

Your positioning in the market is subject to evolution over time but, for the most part, it should remain fairly consistent.

As you've learned by now, I work with entrepreneurial business leaders who want and need to get more leads and sales from the Internet. Occasionally, I'll add that I focus on roofing contractors, attorneys, cosmetic dentists, and chiropractors – but my emphasis is always on helping the owners of businesses improve revenue and profits.

If people don't know you, but find themselves in need of your products and services when they come to your website and they still don't clearly understand what you do – you'll lose that sale.

If your positioning isn't clear and someone asks your competitor about you, it's possible the competitor will be able to honestly say, "I'm not really sure if they even offer this service."

Again, you lose.

So – if you haven't already done so, grab that sheet of paper and write down at least five (preferably ten) problems that you solve or results your customers/clients get when they buy your products and services. Then, take a few minutes and research your top competitors' sites, to see how many of them do the same things. When you do this, you'll find a few they either don't do, or some they don't promote in their marketing.

Develop your marketing messages and the content on your site to speak directly to *their* issues and about the problems that your company can solve that no one else offers. We'll go into this a bit more in-depth soon.

You'll be glad you did this – especially because it will help you stop playing Twister in your marketing and get more ideal clients calling and seeking you out for the unique programs you have.

Now you know the makings of the best possible USP for your business – complete with examples from major rock stars, a sitcom, and a pair of khakis. This will provide you with the ammunition you need to make your business and the value you bring to the table so desirable people will literally ignore the competition and work with you instead – on your terms. Combined with an intimate understanding of precisely who your ideal customers are, you should now be prepared to develop the perfect keywords to help those customers find you. We'll get into that next.

KEYWORD

CHAPTER FIVE

Generating Effective, Targeted Keywords

In this chapter, you will learn:

- Niches of the riches kind

- Getting to the heart of Internet search

- Three steps to ideal keyword selection

- Keyword research...tools and tactics

- It's more than being Number One

- Beware the bargain that isn't

You may already know this – and, if you don't, it's time that you did: No matter what product or service you sell, there are potential buyers waiting for it. It doesn't matter how specialized whatever you sell happens to be, you can now reach out with your message, directed *only* to those people most likely interested in buying, and generate more sales.

This is the essence of niche marketing. It's what Internet lead generation is all about.

Let's pretend for a minute you like to play ping pong. A *lot*. Maybe you don't have to pretend. Even better.

Among your friends at the local bar, you're the king. Sure – you win more than anyone there, but you're absolutely certain it's the limited-edition specially-balanced paddle with the intricately hand-tooled antler handle that gives you that winning edge.

During a heated match for a round of beers, you hit a slam over the net for the win – and slam that beautiful paddle to the table surface in the process. It breaks in half.

Now you need a new paddle. But – how on earth will you *ever* replace it? It was a gift from your father who has passed away and you have no idea where he got it. You could try another one, but you're absolutely certain you'll never win like you used to without *that* paddle.

Would you drive to the local department store and start searching the shelves? Maybe…if you're lucky…there's a large specialty sports store in your area. You might head over there and hope they stock something.

You never know. They might still make ping pong paddles like the one you just broke – or they might not. You could wind up searching store shelves in your town and the three closest to you without success.

Or…would it make more sense to search the Internet and see what's available?

After all – there actually might be a very similar paddle three towns over from you. If you checked the Internet first, you could call and ask them about it, see if there are any in stock, and then drive directly there to get it.

There could be someone selling those very paddles online, shipped to your door.

Yes – this imaginary example's a *bit* extreme. But not as much as you might think. I've often joked that you could probably make a living selling pet tarantula leashes online, with the right Internet marketing in place.

You think I'm kidding? I just did a search on Google for "pet tarantula supplies" and got roughly 171,000 results!

In the end, you might not actually be able to make a *living* selling leashes to fans of these hairy creatures, but it's clear there's a market for them among people who keep them as pets. Who knows? Maybe now you're pumped to try selling some. Consider it a free business idea from me – just let me know how it works out.

This plays directly to the heart of what Internet search is all about and why so many people today look online first for whatever it is they feel will solve their current problem. It doesn't matter whether it's a need for a championship ping pong paddle, everything needed to keep a pet tarantula happy – or whatever it is *you* sell.

Keep in mind – of those people who have an interest in what you do, almost all of them (+/- 90%) will start their search on the Internet when they consider buying your "thing."

More interesting; most sales are triggered by a problem consumers want to solve. This leads them to start looking for solutions (not necessarily solutions to *buy* – not right away, anyway).

They go online to look for those solutions and they search for them with "keywords" – the "hook" upon which SEO hangs its hat. These keywords are the specific words and phrases people tend to enter into a search engine when they're looking for the right solution to their needs.

To maximize sales and lead generation online, you want to identify the precise words or phrases the type of people you most want to attract to your business would enter into a search engine when they're searching for a solution to the specific problems you can help them solve.

Get the keywords rollin'...

There are three basic things you need to do, to select the best keywords on which you need to focus your efforts:

1. *Keyword selection.* The specific words and phrases people are searching for related to the product or services your business sells.
2. *Advanced keyword research.* Analyzing which of the words and phrases you've identified will generate the most profit for you, if you rank highly for them.

3. *Skip keywords with huge monthly search traffic.* If this sounds a little counter-intuitive, consider this: if thousands upon thousands of people are searching on a keyword each month, the competition you'll have to battle to rank highly for that term can be *fierce*. If, instead, you identify keywords with less competition, but still plenty of active searches, then create pages for several of them, you can still generate *loads* of traffic without the heavy competition.

To identify the best keywords to focus on for your business, turn to your description of the ideal client or customer you identified. Imagine you are one of these people.

This shouldn't be too hard. You just imagined you were a ping-pong champion. I saw you!

If you have any problem with this…go back and re-read the chapter on identifying your ideal customer and determining your USP. Pretend you're a big movie star (hey…admit it…you do this now and then already – it's ok, we *all* do every once in a while). You're about to be called to the set and the character you're playing is your ideal customer.

For a moment, close your eyes and *become* that person. It's kind of like method acting. Don't worry. This isn't painful and you can switch back at any time.

Ask yourself what problem that person would have that you could solve with what you sell. *Picture* this person having that problem. *See* them sitting down at the computer, bringing up a search engine, then typing in…what?

Let's say you *do* sell tarantula leashes. Would you type in "pet tarantula supplies?" *Maybe*. But, as I pointed out, that got me 171,000 results and included things like spider food, setting up a terrarium, and a lot of other topics. "Tarantula" or "leash" would be far more competitive and unproductive but – what about "tarantula leash" or "spider leash?"

Even better…what about "tarantula exercise," "exercising a pet tarantula," or even "keeping a pet tarantula from getting lost"?

Hey! I said I know the example's kind of extreme, but…this really is what you need to do with your ideal customer in mind. Sometimes, the ideal keyword is sitting there, hardly touched by the competition because they didn't think it would ever see much traffic and didn't do the research you did.

In the end, you want to build a list of at least the *five* keywords you think are associated most closely with what your business sells. But…don't type them directly into a search engine to see how competitive they are. Instead, you can gain a lot of actionable information about which keywords are being searched and by how many people with one of these tools:

1. *Google Keyword Planner* – This is provided by Google for use with Google's AdWords PPC programs (their paid advertising platform), but it provides valuable keyword usage information for your SEO, too. It's also free to use and very useful. With this free tool, you can see how many people search each month for keywords

that match what you're doing. It will also show you how many companies are competing for each term.

2. *Market Samurai* – I've used this fairly low-cost tool for keyword research for several years now and I find it to be incredibly valuable. You can learn more about it and get a free trial to test it out by visiting: http://bit.ly/ms0813.

The name of the game is to decide on just five keywords – ten at most – that a reasonable number of people are searching for, but with low enough competition that you've got a decent chance to rank highly for them.

For my own clients, I tend to work mostly with keywords that get 30-50 "exact" searches per day. This means the searcher typed that word or phrase into the search engine *exactly* as you're using it.

For example: you'll see different results for "furniture moving" vs "moving furniture." You want to optimize for the *exact* term, as opposed to a "broad" match, which can include misspellings, synonyms, related searches, and other possibly (but not always) relevant variations.

It's not uncommon to eventually add dozens of SEO landing pages to your site to attract prospects, if not more, but I always focus my efforts on *exact* match keywords.

Beware the unbelievable bargain…

This isn't all that difficult, but it most certainly can require a bit of time and effort. Putting together the various pages for the keywords and optimizing those pages can also be a considerable amount of work.

The effort's *very* worthwhile – but you might not have much choice in the matter. After all – chances are good you already have your hands full running your business.

It's tempting to hire some outside help with this. If you don't feel you're up to the task, I recommend you do. However, watch out for deals that are obviously too good to be true. Emails guaranteeing they can get you to number one on Google for just $97 a month arrive in my "in" box all the time. Most likely, you get them, too.

It might sound like such a good deal you'd be a fool to pass it up.

It's not…and you're not. Here's why:

As you know by now – this kind of stuff makes me cringe whenever I hear it! Business owners often hear legendary tales of SEO success – it seems everyone knows the name of the game is to be found at the top of the listings in Google.

As I already pointed out earlier, even being found on the first *page* of Google for a search isn't enough – unless you've taken some important first steps.

1. If you're found on page one of Google for keywords no one is searching for, you'll get zero traffic to your site.
2. If you're found on page one of Google for important keywords, but you aren't in the top three spots, the amount of resulting traffic you get will be small. Over

70% of people searching online for something will click on one of the top three listings. The next 20% of searches are divided among those listed numbers four through ten. This isn't too great for you, if you're number eight.

You also need to understand that it's *Google* who decides who shows up where, based on the search engine's proprietary formula for ranking websites. As I'm writing this, they were reportedly measuring over 200 different elements when making that decision.

I'm explaining this so you'll understand – someone who has the skills to manually work on your website's pages and improve them until they're at the top of the results can't possibly do what you need for a price that's *too* low. Much of this takes some time to map out and implement. $97 for a number one ranking – or even to show up on page one – is simply...*really* – too good to be true.

Perhaps there are companies that *can* do it, but I don't see how it's possible and I haven't found one yet. I'll keep you posted...but don't hold your breath.

Usually, people who promote offers like this are overseas workers. This can certainly lower the cost to provide the extensive services required to actually perform on the promise.

I've hired lots of overseas help before, too – but, when it comes to sensitive, potentially high-value work, you want someone who is US-based – someone who can *explain* what they're doing – especially if something goes wrong.

If you hire a worker in India or Pakistan to do your SEO work, they can't be held accountable for the work they're doing for you. Believe me – this is *one* case where you want to work with someone you can understand clearly and who understands you clearly when you have a question. Someone who, preferably, operates under the jurisdiction of the country in which you live.

Don't fall victim to a scam which, in the end, won't help you at all – unless you simply have so much extra cash you need help disposing of some. As I walk you through the rest of the steps in this process, you'll be able to make an intelligent decision about how to proceed and who best to hire to handle it, if you can't.

For now – get into "method acting mode." Become your very best premium customer, looking for a solution to that person's unique problems. Get the right keywords sorted out and you'll be armed and ready to launch an SEO or a PPC campaign with a reasonable expectation of success.

We'll go deeper into what you need to put those keywords to work building up some traffic with SEO. First, I feel it's important that you see how the research you've done so far can pay off quickly with PPC.

You now know the true power behind finding your perfect niche. Match this to your USP, armed with a profile of your perfect customer, and you can start lining out keywords for an SEO or PPC campaign designed to deliver new prospective clients and customers to your door. You also know why SEO isn't about being "number one," and you know how to spot an apparent "bargain" that really isn't one, should you run into it during the process. You should now be ready to dive into PPC some more and the first step is getting the right landing pages ready. I'll cover that next.

CHAPTER SIX

PPC Landing Page Concepts

In this chapter, you will learn:

- When less can be more
- Sending prospects to the right page
- The elements of a solid PPC landing page
- Avoiding Google's "stupid tax"
- Why WordPress is your PPC friend
- One page will never do

"In Judges 15:16, Samson said, 'With a donkey's jawbone I have killed a thousand men.' *Ten times* that many sales are killed every day with the *exact* same weapon, across this country alone."

Those were the words of my sales manager, in response to my question, "How did I do?"

It was the first time he'd gone with me on an appointment, to see a customer.

Needless to say, I didn't make the sale.

Perhaps you can remember a time when something like that happened to you. I bring this up because, if your main website is part of your sales process, I'm certain this is happening to you regularly. You might not have to stare into an online visitor's eyes while you hear the word "no," but they're still saying it – more often than you think.

Like – every day. Perhaps even right now. And you don't even know it.

They're saying it because, on your site, you're saying the wrong things or – worse – making statements on your lead generation pages that go beyond what's necessary for maximum conversions. In short, talking too much.

This is even more important for you to keep in mind as you start planning and designing lead generation pages for PPC campaigns.

I've already talked about the importance of attracting ideal customers or clients while simultaneously repelling those who aren't ideal for your business. I've also gone over developing an "avatar" of an ideal client and I explained how this exercise will make you much more effective in your marketing.

I've taken you through this process to show you the importance of studying your best clients and truly understanding what specifically makes them ideal. This is a vital exercise when it comes to determining the best search terms on which to rank with your SEO. It's life-or-death when you start paying for PPC traffic. However – it's equally important that you pay attention to who your less-than-ideal clients are, so you can develop an approach that helps fend them off as you attract your ideal.

You need to do this because less-than-ideal clients can make your life more miserable than you might ever imagine. They generally haggle over your going rates and will tend to nickel-and-dime you to death on every billing – or they consistently demand more attention than other clients for the money they do pay. Or both.

Consider what these less-than-ideal clients are *really* looking for, as opposed to those you'd most like to attract. There *are* subtle differences and, sometimes, you'll need to climb into both ways of thinking to ferret them out.

For example, if you focus only on low prices or discount offers, you'll find you tend to attract clients and customers focused on price as the main benefit they're seeking. These are rarely the easiest customers to work with.

Likewise, discount offers and sales, while they can help boost sales in the short term, will also tend to bring you clientele focused primarily on price, unless you offer those discounts or sales *after* having already firmly established the real-world value of what you offer. These won't be your ideal customers, either. Bargain-seekers don't usually appreciate the value of what you offer and will make your life less than desirable in the process.

It's easy to fall into this trap as you plan out your PPC campaign and the landing page you'll send that traffic to visit.

You want to encourage visitors to take action fast and the tendency is to "make them an offer they can't refuse." Sadly, you'll also often wind up attracting clientele you wish you *had* refused, if you don't take the right approach with the offer you make here.

You might be faced with competition bragging about lower prices and selling the same or similar products or services as you do. Surprisingly, in this case, if you focus instead on the higher quality of your service after the sale, the higher quality of what you sell, or other benefits of buying from you, you'll find you can even charge *more* than your competitors and attract a better grade of customer when you do.

Keep these considerations in mind as you plan your PPC landing page. You'll then attract the type of clients you dream of having – people you most enjoy working with, who appreciate you for the added value you bring to the table and reward you with their repeat business and referrals to like-minded new clients and customers. You'll enjoy what you do more and your life will be much better as a result.

MAKE IT CLEAR TO PROSPECTIVE CLIENTS THAT YOU'RE SELECTIVE IN WHO YOU WORK WITH.

~ Scott A. Dennison

Now you're in the right mindset, ready to put together the different web pages you'll need to make your PPC campaigns generate an excellent ROI for your dollar.

When you take all that ideal client "stuff" and bake it into the words on these PPC landing pages – when it's clear to visitors that you're selective in who you work with – then, ideally, you'll get more of the kind of customers you prefer and less of those you don't.

You'll also kill a *lot* less of the sales you most want to make.

First things first – when someone clicks on your ad, what page/website are you going to send them to visit?

You might have spent a ton of money on a slick-looking, informative website. You might, for this reason, feel this would be the perfect place to send your AdWords traffic and draw in customers.

I agree this sounds reasonable enough – in theory. Unfortunately, it's actually the *wrong* approach.

Believe it or not, you're far more likely to <u>lose</u> clients if you're routing all your ad traffic to your main website!

Please re-read the above paragraph. Out loud. Then highlight it and read it again in a day or so, so you never ever forget that thought again.

You *must* send AdWords traffic to a landing page *specifically designed* to match up with the ad that sent people there. Yes – it needs to be one of those single-page, simple, easy-to-read landing pages that invites the prospect to take action *now*.

The simplest of these pages include only a paragraph or two of text below an eye-catching headline. Both lead directly from the specific ad that brought the visitor to that page. There's also usually an opt in-form or a link to a form or some other call to action on the page – and usually an arrow or other eye-catching graphic pointing to the action element.

It's direct marketing, pure and simple. It *must* be.

These landing pages get the person who clicked on your ad involved right away, so they contact you *before* they get distracted by anything else.

If your traffic from your AdWords campaign is being routed to your main website, you run a constant risk of visitors getting distracted by all the different sections on your site. They're likely to take no action at all. Even if they wind up really liking your page and bookmark it to read in-depth later, they didn't pick up the phone. They didn't fill out a contact form. They aren't a lead for new business and might *never* be.

You just *lost* a potential client. And you *paid* for the "privilege" of doing so.

If the landing page is written properly and the call to action is compelling and clear enough, however, you'll get people converting. They'll call you and come into your business. They'll take the action you wanted them to take. In other words, you'll start generating leads.

I'm frequently asked, "Why create a landing page, if I already have a website?"

The #1 trap Google has placed in the path of their customers/advertisers is how they handle processing the traffic they send them. There's a concept widely talked about by the people who advertise on Google. It's known as Google's "stupidity tax."

This stems from:

1) the keywords you're using and
2) how you process the traffic they send you

If you do a poor job at keyword selection – if your keywords are already broad, for example, or if you don't include negative keywords (keywords you specifically want to exclude) – you'll pay a fortune in advertising costs for traffic that will rarely, if ever, buy from you. So, you want to first get the right keywords, format them properly and then send them to a landing page.

The reason for the landing page? The person who clicked on your ad was searching for something *very* specific. You want to keep them, so you need to match precisely what they were searching for on that page. This allows us to focus the mind of the consumer around the unique client proposition and call to action you want them to take while they're there.

If you send them to your home page and the visitor has to figure out where they can find the info they were just looking for, they'd rather simply back out and go elsewhere. By using a landing page, we can focus them and keep them right on the topic they were interested in, enabling them to make the decision to inquire / take action.

Once you have your keywords – including negative keywords – selected and formatted properly, and your landing page is set up, you're going to see an increasing and steady amount of AdWords traffic visiting the page. It's pretty amazing, actually. Kind of like a spigot – you can open it up and get as much traffic as you want/need or are willing to pay for whenever you want, simply by turning your campaign "on" or "off." Ideally, it can pay for itself, so you can simply continue to reinvest and keep it rolling.

A good example is an attorney client I'm working with. I showed him how, over the last three months, he'd spent about $2,500 in ads. What he got in return was a combination of lead forms and phone calls through a tracking phone number we set up. He got a total of 30 leads.

His response to that was, "If I sell two of those 30, I'm profitable."

Get this – the typical number, in his case, is to sell one in *three*. If his "typical" numbers hold – and the proper keyword targeting and landing page setup will help make that happen – he'd sell *10* of those 30 leads! This AdWords campaign can be *massively* profitable for him.

His only response was, "How can we expand and do more?"

The answer is equally straightforward: he now only needs to increase his budget to get more business.

The light was on. He was responding to the fact that, if an investment of $2,500 will net 30 chances to close new clients, we just need to spend more and get more.

This should be your response, too.

As the traffic comes in, you'll also see all kinds of opportunities to optimize the campaign. Many, many advertisers on Google set it up and forget about it. They either don't have the skills or they're lazy and don't take the time to monitor the campaign, to look for ways to improve it. These are generally the same people who will, in the end, tell you that AdWords doesn't work after they've given it a try.

Instead, we monitor the campaigns on a weekly basis. We split test, to improve the ads themselves, also improving the click-thru rates on the ads, and we improve the landing page, based on the traffic coming in.

All along the way, we also apply the 80/20 Rule to our analysis, to show us what gets tossed and what should receive more attention.

One of my clients was advertising on his own. Every time someone clicked on his ad, it was costing him about $40. It was clearly hurting him, because he couldn't get enough opportunities out of that to get his money off the table. We took over and started monitoring and optimizing the campaign by increasing his click-thru rate. His cost per click fell thru the floor, dropping his costs drastically. What he was spending $40 on before was now costing him $12 – and providing him with three and a half to four times as many opportunities to close a sale for the same money.

The combination of the right keywords, sent to a professionally-developed landing page, generates traffic from AdWords. By optimizing those campaigns on a regular basis and refining the landing page and call to action itself, we begin to see steady growth in the lead flow.

WordPress development/content development/clear call to action...

We've briefly discussed generating leads with AdWords. We'll get into it some more a bit later but, to get there, we also have to build an effective lead generation website.

I've been around the Internet since 1998 and I can recall the progression websites have gone through. Once, people thought it was neat to be able to put up a website so everyone could find it. Pretty quickly, the standard business website evolved into a brochure on the Internet people could access from anywhere.

This was what came to be referred to – after Web 2.0 was established – as Web 1.0. Before that...it was just "The web."

Web 2.0 was establish as websites evolved into tools to be used for conducting conversations with people. This is when sites were designed to attract people to our own spot on the web, to have a dialog with them, to talk with them, to answer their questions, and so forth. This brought on the "social media" phase we have today.

Although we don't really need to go into the social media scene here, the mindset that the web is a living thing that we can use as a tool for communication is very prevalent in what I'm about to explain: it's my philosophy behind using the web.

The idea is to build a customized, attractive website but, more important, it's going to be designed *specifically* to do what you it want it to do – to generate leads.

For a whole lot of reasons, we no longer build websites with HTML – the "coding" language of the Internet. There are some people who still do, but it's the most complicated way to go these days. It's now far better to build websites on a dynamic platform, rather than a static, straight-up "HTML" format that comes closer to producing those web "billboards" of old.

WordPress is one of the most popular and powerful dynamic website platforms today. It's often referred to as a content management system. The beauty of using a dynamic platform such as WordPress is that all the information that lives on your website – the pictures, the words, everything about your site – actually lives inside a database. There's also an exterior to a WordPress Website, referred to as a "theme" or "skin," that controls how the site looks.

The beauty of this arrangement is that we can update the theme from time to time, completely changing the site's look very quickly. We can also easily change the content on the site, without having to rebuild it when we do. Everything's in the database. The site is only actually generated whenever someone visits the web address. Each visitor sees the latest version of the site that's generated for them from the database when they arrive, including any of the changes you've made when they do. You only update what you want to.

The biggest advantage to a WordPress site, then, is flexibility. It's also an extremely inexpensive platform that provides a fast turnaround to implementation. Sites can be built quickly, then easily optimized for better search engine visibility and you don't have to learn a bunch of complicated code to do it. We're going to take advantage of all of that with the process I'm laying out for you here.

With the keywords we've developed, we then engage in this process of WordPress development/content development/on-page optimization/call to action. Those are all the components, or ingredients, of a lead generation website.

With the right foundational preparation – creating a solid USP, keywords, and branding – you can then use a formula to develop a very straightforward website that speaks to the ideal client or customer, communicates your USP, and asks them to take action on that USP, to choose you or to take the first step, whatever you determine that should be.

With WordPress, getting the framework up and running usually takes just a few days. After a bit of customization of the look of the site and fine-tuning some stuff along the way, you move to the next step: developing the content.

An ideal landing page for PPC should include, then, only information directly related to the search term or terms you're using to attract clicks that send people to that particular page. This information doesn't necessarily have to be revealed on the landing page itself. Your landing page can be a link to the specific information being sought – and the "answer" could be filling out a brief subscription form to join your email list, after which you'll send the information they wanted to see.

Overall, PPC marketing is two-step direct marketing, in its purest form, directed at a precise targeted audience seeking an answer to a specific question.

You might, for example, offer *one* solution directly related to the search term or terms…and an invitation to the visitor to sign up for your list for similar, even *better* tips. You could also then include a teaser or two as to what additional answers the visitor can expect after opting in. Then, in the emails you send to list members, fulfilling the promise you made when they signed up, keep mentioning that you can save them a tremendous amount of time and – surprisingly – money when they choose to have you do it all for them instead.

If you provide services performed for clients, you can also do well with a landing page that shows people step-by-step how to do what you do for them on their own. Point out how much less time-consuming this same process can be when the visitor enlists some affordable help…then invite the visitor to join your list to find out how they can make this process happen with the best results possible – by hiring *you*.

The key to a great PPC landing page is keeping it short and simple, directly on-point with answers to the specific question or questions a visitor had in mind when he or she typed in the search term that brought them to your ad. By "simple," I mean you should maintain a steady focus on a "less is good" approach.

One powerful way to tie your PPC ads directly to a landing page, for example, would be to create an ad that asks a question or that starts a statement directly related to the targeted search term – and the answer or the *rest* of the statement is on the landing page people see when they click – perhaps in the headline they see the moment the page opens. The ad itself might say, "An easy garment waterproofing solution," for example. The landing page, then, could lead right into one powerfully quick way the visitor can waterproof their own garments, along with an invitation to get even *more* tips by signing up to join your list.

You've heard of "Johnny one-note." Your PPC landing pages should each be "Johnny one-topic," with a different page for every topic to which your targeted keywords apply. Don't clutter the page up with *anything* other than what's necessary to tie that page directly to the specific keyword that brought visitors there. Add a specific reason or reasons why they simply must click the button to book a call with you now and get rid of *everything* else that might stand in the way of or distract from visitors taking that action.

I often use professional writers who work with all the keywords I'm trying to optimize the site around, along with the framework of what the story needs to say. The writer then creates the articles or content for placement on the site.

You want your writers, whoever you use, to create the highest quality content, because Google has made it very clear they want to present the highest quality results to people who are searching. To the degree that you can, if your desire is to be the number one Website in the world for a keyword, you should come as close as you can to presenting the world with the best page with the best information related to that keyword that you can.

You might be thinking, "How do I do that?" It's not as hard as it might sound. You simply look at who's ahead of you in the rankings for that keyword now, see what type of content they're putting out, and present better information than they are, relating to that keyword.

This is well worth whatever extra effort might be required. It can be the "make or break" element for any PPC campaign.

Google developed a formula as an update to their existing algorithm, so it's "just an update" – but it was a huge shift in how Google ranked pages before. They called this update "Panda." In literal terms, it's a filter and its job is to filter out poor quality content. For this reason, when Google sends their virtual "spiders" to crawl your content on your site, we want them to say, "That content is extremely relevant to the keyword and is worthy of being indexed and presented."

By itself, this isn't enough – but it does form the basis of where you want to start. It's why you want to do what's necessary to create great content for these pages.

A magazine publisher I know once told me, sighing deeply, with the kind of look in his eyes usually reserved for losing a loved one, "I wish I had all the checks possible subscribers have stuck on their fridges with magnets, but never got around to putting in an envelope and mailing to me."

When the work identifying the precise keywords to attract your ideal clients is done, and you've designed your campaign to drive those people you most desire to reach to your landing page, you want *nothing* to get in the way of the action you want people to take after clicking on that ad. You don't want them to wind up stuck up on the fridge.

As for the design of your page itself, a solidly-converting landing page is specifically designed using a proven template to get your prospects to do *one* thing. What that one thing is might vary – you might want visitors to pick up the phone and call you, you may want them to set an appointment on an online calendar so you can call *them*, or you might want them to fill out a form to receive a free newsletter or to sign up for special "members-only style" discounts, a special report, or a free ebook. It's up to you and your audience what works best here. Split-testing different enticements will show you which items your ideal clients respond to best. The ever-powerful 80/20 Rule will help you determine the winners and losers.

Plan to set up more than one landing page and more than one ad going to each of those pages. Google lets you set up multiple ads and automatically rotate them, so split-testing becomes automatic, once you've this set up the way you want and turn it on.

The key, again, is designing your ads so they attract the right kind of targeted lead to a *specific* page that's only designed to capture the lead you'd most like to see come in. Because you have only a limited number of words in an AdWords ad and you want to also "close the deal" on your landing page with the fewest words possible, you'll find that the use of multiple landing pages, to rotate in and out with multiple ads, will help you quickly "dial in" and find the right combination for maximum click-through rate (CTR).

This takes some effort and then some trial-and-error after you start getting traffic…but it's required effort that will help you generate results you can quickly see.

> *We've now covered the elements of a solid PPC landing page and I've shown you how to avoid the dreaded Google "stupid tax," keeping the cost of clicks you buy at their lowest. I've also pointed out why one PPC landing page is not like the others, so you need multiple pages for maximum results – and how to send the right prospects to the best page for them. I also showed you how you could be sending people away with what you say – and how to know when enough is enough. Next: I'll walk you through turning your main website into the best possible SEO magnet it can be.*

CHAPTER
SEVEN

Designing Your Website to Generate *and* Convert Leads

In this chapter, you will learn:

- Why "pretty" won't help you

- A place for every page

- Setting the right "bait" for conversions

- Showing, not selling

We've already discussed why you don't want to send AdWords clicks to your company website. Any page to which you send AdWords PPC clicks should be *specifically* designed to match the ad that sent the click and, in the process, to capture a lead – clean and simple. It's always a good idea to enlist the aid of a competent online business lead and conversion specialist with this process, if at all possible.

Don't panic. Your main business website is still valuable. After all – it's your online "company store." Even better, this is also where you can put SEO into action, for longer-term results. This way, you can make certain your company website generates and converts leads, in addition to your PPC landing pages. More of a good thing is always better, right?

Although you don't send AdWords clicks directly to this main site, people will visit it as a result of your SEO and other marketing efforts. After people click on your PPC ad, then visit your opt-in page, for example, they could also visit your main site – whether they've opted in or not – to find out more about you. This can present you with another excellent opportunity to turn those visitors into additional leads for your business.

Pretty has its place...

To get this right, you don't really want to involve your web designer. I'm sure you were taught growing up to always include everyone. However, website designers – regardless of what they might tell you – are primarily focused on making your site *pretty*. While pretty might get a lady more dates, it won't get you more leads. This is why an online lead generation and conversion specialist can best help you take these vital next steps and turn your company site into the best lead generation and conversion machine it can be.

I'm not saying you can't do this yourself. You *do*, however, need to understand what you're doing and what's required, to meet or exceed your goals.

Most of my clients would rather leave this part of the equation up to a specialist. The choice, of course, is yours.

You want to start by making certain your main website navigation is structured properly. This is the first step in turning your main site into something more than simply another static billboard on the wide open information superhighway.

The diagram, below, will illustrate what I mean.

Your "most important" pages should all be linked *directly* from the home page of your site. Your most important pages are usually either your different content category pages or your product category (money) pages. Maybe both.

Then you link the individual posts or pages in the next tier down. Often, these consist of your individual SKU's, or product information pages.

You'll see an example in this diagram:

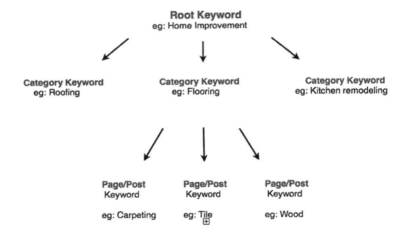

For SEO purposes, you'll want to have the search engines index your relevant pages. Any pages that are more than two clicks removed from the home page won't be indexed, so these won't be found in the search results.

Ensure that your navigation is structured properly and that your money (sales) pages and posts are stationed where they will be indexed.

To find out what's indexed on your site now and as you continue through this process, go to Google and, in the search box, type:

[site:http://yoursite.com]

Note: in the above example, insert *your* site's url, after the word "site:"

And then there's conversion...

Following the steps I've outlined so far, you should now be ready to put SEO to work, to do its thing and bring you even more leads. This will help turn your main business page into an attractive beacon to the search engines, so they know what traffic you're looking for and start sending it your way.

You also now understand that traffic is traffic...nothing more, nothing less. That's why you want to do all you can to convert those new visitors to your site into leads. Until they become a lead, they're just more traffic and bragging rights never buys the groceries.

Once again, the thinking you've done to map out exactly who your ideal customer is will provide tremendous help here. You'll want to crawl into the mind of that perfect new client again and think like he or she does, to determine the perfect enticement you could offer your new visitors that will lure them into opting in, to join your list and hear more from you.

Picture your target – the perfect new customer you most want to attract – sitting in a straight-backed chair facing you, glaring at you with a scowl, arms crossed. For a moment, you can hear in your head what he or she is thinking:

"I don't know who you are. I don't know your company. I don't know your company's products. I don't know what your company stands for. I don't know your company's customers. I don't know your company's record. I don't know your company's reputation. Now – what was it you wanted to sell me?"

The scene I just painted was depicted brilliantly in a full-page ad designed by the late, great advertising legend, David Ogilvy. The ad appeared decades ago, in *Advertising Age* magazine, to illustrate the kind of resistance excellent marketing must overcome. It's an ad he ran to attract new clients to his advertising agency and it's as valid today as it ever was.

Your prospective customers – especially new visitors to your website – will rarely make a snap decision to buy. In most cases, you'll need to take your newfound traffic through a process of persuasion.

It's easy to fall through that trap door known as the ego here. Most business owners do. After all – from your viewpoint, you have the best of whatever it is you sell and provide the best possible service when someone buys. All you should need to do is get people to see that and sales will flow.

Right?

Wrong.

Remember – new visitors to your
site clicked *one* link among a list
of many on a search engine. They
got to your page but, to them,
you're still anonymous…an
unknown entity. Going for a sale
at this moment is like asking
someone on a date without first
even knowing their name.

Going for a sale when someone visits
your site for the first time
is like asking someone on a date
without first even knowing their name.

~ Scott A. Dennison

They could say, "Yes…" but the odds are high that's not the
answer you'll hear.

Think about the problem or question your new site visitors
most likely have. Decide what it is you could provide to your
new visitors that will most likely solve that problem or
answer those questions immediately – then provide
immediate access to that, in return for the visitor's name and
email address.

This could be an eBook, special access to limited-edition items
as soon as they arrive, unadvertised discounts and specials…a
free phone consultation to answer their questions.

Make sure you add an opt-in form or link to it on your main
page offering this in a way that's difficult for visitors to miss.
Usually, this is best located "above the fold" – a term we use
for the part of your web page that first appears when it opens,
without needing to scroll down to find it.

Your site will naturally provide details about you and your company…possibly an overview of the products and/or services that you sell (with links to deeper pages with more detailed descriptions of each). It most likely already does.

You'll also want to add some more useful information that you know your ideal clients and customers will appreciate having access to. Update them on new happenings in your industry. Provide them with your latest tips and ideas for putting the products or services that you sell to use. Present them with case histories of successful clients. Pull back the curtains and show visitors your operation from the inside out, introducing them to the other people in your company, "behind the screen," so to speak. Give visitors the benefit of your expertise right there on your site and update all of it regularly.

Make every one of these pieces useful, helpful information. Always – always – stress in each piece that, by opting in to your list, the reader will also get "this and this and this" or "this"…and point them to your opt-in offer.

When you do this, you *show* your new site visitors that you're someone they should get to know better with the content you provide on your page and you provide visitors with plenty of reasons to opt in.

Now your main web site will help you attract more traffic *and* convert more of those visitors into qualified leads, to generate more business.

Now you understand why pretty's nice for getting dates, but essentially useless when it comes to SEO on your website. You also know how your website's pages should be organized, for maximizing SEO – and the right "bait" to set in the conversion "trap" you should place on those pages. I've also discussed the power of showing – not selling – to keep visitors on your site longer and make more conversions happen. This means you're now ready to get your SEO set up and rolling in new leads that convert into increased revenue – which we'll dive into next chapter.

SEO PART ONE

CHAPTER EIGHT

SEO Part One:
Optimizing the Right Content

In this chapter, you will learn:

- Listening to your market pays

- Content that compels

- Tagging your pages for SEO results

- Expect to pay for SEO

- Avoiding over-optimization

- Be seen...EVERYWHERE

"Leno, Letterman, and Conan O'Brien aren't as funny as you trying to make a sale."

That's what my friend and associate (now a well-known author and speaker), Jeffrey Gitomer, said to me one day, in 1997.

I'd asked him his opinion on the best way for me to sell more tickets for his live events. I'd spent several years traveling and training sales people, but the purpose for my being in whatever city I was in was to sell tickets to an upcoming seminar with a professional speaker – like Gitomer, Tom Hopkins, or the late Jim Rohn.

So, I asked Jeffrey, "How should I go about improving my ticket sales?"

His answer?

"Buy a tape recorder and record every talk you give, then listen to it again and again, to hear what you sound like making your presentations. I'll bet that Leno, Letterman, and Conan O'Brian – combined – aren't as funny as you trying to close the sale."

Nice…

Sadly, he was right. I *did* record every talk for almost two years. And I listened to them in my car as I was leaving one presentation to go to the next.

In the process, I got very, very good at making those presentations and closing more ticket sales.

EFFECTIVE SEO IS PRETTY EASY.

A few things done in the right order with consistency can make a HUGE difference.

~ Scott A. Dennison

The reason I'm telling you this is because the same thing probably applies to you, if I were to analyze the SEO work currently on your company's web site.

Especially if you did the work yourself.

Or – sad but all too often true – if

you hired someone who used some slick language to convince you they knew what to do, but later proved they didn't know at all.

The truth is that effective SEO is pretty easy. A few things done in the right order with consistency can make a *huge* difference. Truly *listening* to what you're telling your best customers and clients, again and again, can provide countless clues to the best SEO approach for you.

My clients can testify to this.

However, most business owners (probably including you) are experts at their craft and much too busy doing what they do best to learn how to do their own search engine optimization, too.

This is most likely not something you normally do or have ever done before. Even if you've actually optimized your pages for SEO before – more than once – it's likely you still need to "listen to the tapes" several times, going back over everything again and again, to make sure you're getting it right.

Keep this in mind as I run you through this. If it sounds like too much to take on yourself, I understand. If you don't feel compelled to put in the time to learn how this part of lead generation works, there's no shame in admitting you need help with something along the road to success.

Self-made successes are far more rare than you might think.

Still, it's important that you understand the process – even if you decide to hire outside help to handle your SEO work. This will help you see the scams and schemes when they appear at your door and know when to keep looking for someone who *really* knows what they're doing.

Optimizing for maximum results...

If, after checking, you find that some of your money pages aren't getting indexed by the search engines, this is a sign. It's telling you that you still need to optimize your pages. It's an indication there's some confusion, in the eyes of the search engines, as to what the page is about.

This is when you're going to want to understand and apply the principles of *on-page SEO* to the pages and posts on your site.

Most of what you'll read about this topic is wrong. Contrary to popular opinion, search engines like Google have gotten very good at understanding what your page is about. Still, there's no downside to giving them a *little* help. The right level of optimization will help ensure your pages are indexed and that the listings you earn as a result say what you hoped they would.

You have to exercise some care here, because there's also a way you can overdo optimization. This can wind up getting you penalized.

In almost every case, you'll want to focus each post or page around only *one* primary keyword. It's also fairly common to optimize for a secondary keyword – on some pages, but not necessarily on all of them.

One common mistake is forgetting that you still want to engage people with your site content. The best way to do that is to start out with a powerful headline. Headlines ensure that people will *read* your pages and it's often a reason that content gets shared with others. Sharing helps your SEO rankings, too.

We know, for example, that Google's number one most important element on any page is what's called the "Meta Title Tag," or just the title tag, for short. They look at the title tag and compare it to other elements within the page. It tells their computerized arachnids crawling your site what the page is about, without actually having a human look at it. This helps them index the page properly and put it in the right place in their search results.

If you think about it, a typical Google search starts when somebody types in a word or phrase. In a few micro-seconds, Google's able to figure out the 1,000 best pages that are the most accurate results for that search, then sort them and present them to you on your screen, in order of their relevance, from number 1 to 1,000.

The reality of it is that the number of people who go beyond the first 10 results Google shows to them are few. Almost all the interest goes to the people located in the top *three* positions. There's a lot of complexity that goes along with that, but we aren't going to deal with that here. Google's ranking formulas are, after all, changing constantly. It doesn't make sense to immortalize what's going on right now in a book as it will likely be outdated by the time this sees publication. Still, the general principles of what Google is looking for haven't changed much and it's doubtful they will. They're just getting better and better at honing down to exactly that and nothing more.

The point is this: we're going to give them great content. We're going to optimize it properly with the correct title tags – a very compelling title tag – and we're going to have professionally written Meta descriptions.

When you hear the words "Meta description," I want you think in word pictures of a Google search. See the different listings on the search results page for the word representing whatever you were looking for. There's a bold blue link at the top that you click on to get to the page. *That's* your title tag. The words underneath that link are the Meta description you provided. This isn't a *big* part of what Google is using to rank the website, but it *does* have a valuable role: it's the "ad" you're actually presenting to the public when they find your listing with their search. You're trying to sell the public, to get them to click on your link, instead of the one above or below it. This "ad" should be designed to help do that.

If possible, include your primary target keyword for the page in your headline. When it comes to on-page SEO, the most important place for you to include your primary keyword is in the HTML "title" tag.

To view this tag, you need to look in the page's HTML source code. The tag looks something like this:

<title>your keyword phrase</title>.

It's also still very common to include your primary keyword in:

- The Meta description tag. You can include a sentence of description about your site that you'd like the search engines to use in your listing. Including your primary target keyword in this description adds some serious punch to your on-page SEO.

- The Header tags (H1, H2, H3). Although you really only actually need one of these, adding your primary target keyword here will add more SEO "zing."

- The body copy. Use this sparingly. Do *not* focus on "keyword density" in your content. Writing your site content to intentionally include your keyword as many times as possible will get you penalized. This is still being taught by some outdated or outright unscrupulous supposed marketing "experts," but it's also one of those things that now constitutes over-optimization. If you can logically work your keyword into the body copy…fine. Stop there. But, don't sweat it, as long as the copy itself is relevant to the keyword you're ranking for.

- In link text – internal, pointing to other pages on your site and external, to pages that are off of your site.

- In your images – you can use the keyword in both the image name or in the "alt text" areas. Ensure that the target keyword for your page is used as illustrated in the graph, above, for each of your initial group of keywords.

As you can probably see…there are a few considerations you need to balance, to get your website optimized correctly.

Financial freedom isn't free…

Most entrepreneurs I talk to come to me in love with the idea of SEO. They've heard it's "free." I guess this has become a widespread notion because, unlike advertising on TV, radio, or in the paper, you usually don't have to write checks directly for the links themselves.

If you have the requisite skills to do SEO yourself and you don't count the cost of your time in doing so, then you *might* be able to make a case that SEO's free. Whenever you hear this, however, you're either dealing with someone who doesn't understand that *every* form of marketing has a cost (your time is *never* free), or they're simply being dishonest. SEO *will* cost you – in either time or in money.

Still, most business owners don't have the skills they need to effectively do SEO, even if they have the time. They need to hire someone to do it for them.

SEO, then, isn't free, no matter how you look at it. But – if it's done right, if you work with your business' most important keywords and your site gets ranked near the top of search results – the impact can be dramatic, producing an ROI far in excess of whatever you might see from most other advertising or marketing you could do.

You've seen that SEO boils down to just a few things. It's true. That's why I've split the subject into two separate chapters –

one each for the two things you need to focus on. The next step is creating the content I also went over with you, to build your ranking the right way.

Search engines rank *content*, not websites...

When you think about it, people looking online are usually looking for information that provides them with the answers they needed. Especially when they use the search engines.

When you focus your attention on providing valuable, targeted, informative online content that's properly optimized, you won't have to spend time *or* money chasing new customers. They'll come to *you*.

Give those people visiting your website a reason to reach out to you for more information and a percentage of them will do exactly that.

This is the power of direct marketing via the Internet.

This focus on valuable information will also generate sincere back links – links to your information – from other websites. Other websites like to provide their visitors with valuable information and one of the easiest ways to do this is by pointing to that information *from* their site. This information, when you get this part of SEO right, will be yours. So will the new traffic and better rankings that come along with it.

When these two elements are combined properly, you'll never run short of new clients and customers. Game. Set. Match.

This can be more complicated than you might imagine, however. And the rules are constantly in flux.

Clients of mine know that I talk to them about the content they generate and share pretty much all the time. It's *that* important. People do business with other people. But the key, as I opened this chapter pointing out, is that they do business with people they *know, like*, and *trust*.

If you regularly create and share high-quality, targeted content, people will become familiar with your name. I do this all the time. It's not uncommon for me to meet someone who will remark, "I see you *everywhere!*"

This isn't some happy accident – and, no, it doesn't mean I'm stalking them!

By getting my content out there, I get known. From there, we focus on the liking and trusting part of the equation. Both of these happen faster when ideal client prospects read what I've posted and learn something valuable from it.

Just as it is with almost all aspects of life, if you share or give without thought to what you get in return, you usually receive in abundance. Those who are known as givers are often liked by many, too.

The trust part grows organically. When you share information and ideas with people and do it consistently, people begin to realize that you're for real – someone they should talk with more about providing the solutions they need.

Understanding this, go back to your initial list of keywords and begin creating content that talks about the problems people have that your products/service solve.

The concept is simple, really: seek to create the "best" piece of content on your topic anywhere on the Internet. Search engines and other sites will then *want* people to be able to find it.

Excellent written content is usually lengthy, as much as 1000 words or more. An ideal standard, when creating content that drives your SEO – can't usually be done in 300-500 words.

If *writing* content isn't your thing, consider other types of content, including videos, podcasting, or conducting live webinars or teleseminars.

Another option would be to hire a qualified writer to help you generate excellent content for your prospects to enjoy. You can find decent writers locally by advertising on Craig's List. You can also use services like Textbroker.com or The ContentAuthority.com.

Just remember – don't create content that's intentionally "loaded up" with your keyword repeated all over the place. You want to include your keywords when they apply *directly* to your content and would naturally fit in the conversation where you place them.

At this point in our journey, I've explained to you why it pays to listen to your market. I've shown you the power of compelling content and provided the steps you should follow to properly tag your pages for results from your SEO efforts...including how to avoid over-doing it. You also now understand the power of being seen wherever you can as often as possible. You're ready, then, to move on to the second half of the SEO equation – which is exactly what we'll do, in the next chapter.

SEO PART TWO

CHAPTER NINE

SEO Part Two:
Professional Back-Link Campaigns

In this chapter, you will learn:

- Encouraging quality back-links

- How penguins will affect your future success

- Making the most of your back-links

- Understanding what Google REALLY wants

- Secret social SEO sauce

- Getting the best...or worst...SEO service

Once you have quality internal content optimized on your site, you're ready to share your content with the world. If you've created the best article ever on your topic, *lots* of people will naturally want to link to it and share it with others.

This will create quality back-links to your site, done the right way...something the search engines reward with higher rankings.

Still, you should always be on the lookout for other legitimate ways to add links to your site that will boost its authority in the eyes of the search engines.

This isn't a link-building course. Far from it. In the Google terms of service, we're *not* allowed to build links to our own sites. That said, there *are* legitimate ways of having at least *some* control, when it comes to getting links coming in to your site.

Ten of the most popular back-link-building methods include:

- Submitting guest blog posts to other blogs
- Creating a high-value "lens" on Squidoo.com
- Submitting your blog to directories on http://bestoftheweb.org
- Finding website directories in your niche and submitting your link for inclusion
- Interviewing (and being interviewed by) other bloggers
- Getting clients and friends to link to your site
- Making sure your social profiles (Facebook, Twitter, LinkedIn) include a link to your site
- Adding your blog to different communities on http://blogcarnival.com
- Answering questions for people on sites such as Quora.com
- Starting or participating in forum conversations and linking to your own site in the signature line with your comments

The most powerful ways to naturally *attract* links to your site include:

- Creating "Link Bait" – high-value content that people will naturally want to share
- Hiring a programmer to create a simple piece of software you can give away to visitors (again, people love sharing links to valuable freebies)
- Developing a "badge" for visitors to add to their sites

Here's the thing: the number and quality of the sites that link to your site is a solid indication of your authority and value to your community. But, if you try to build a *ton* of links to your own sites too quickly, Google *will* catch you. When they do, they won't count the links you've built and may, in fact, punish you for doing it.

Worst-case: screw this up and it'll be "No Google for you!"

Watch out for the penguins...

Because people are constantly trying to figure out how to "game" Google, to get top rankings without actually earning them, Google constantly adjusts the algorithms their computers use to generate those rankings.

On April 24, 2012, Google updated their search algorithm to focus on "web spam" issues. I mentioned this earlier. It's known as Google's "Penguin" update. One of the issues addressed in the Penguin update was back-links and the keyword/anchor text used to display your link.

Some years before this update, marketers had discovered that Google relied heavily on back-links, to determine if a site was important enough to rank highly in their listings. Once that was known, the name of the game quickly became "get as many back-links as possible, to improve our chances of being found at the top of search results for our keywords."

Hey – if *some* is good, more is most certainly better, right?

The result? A *lot* of junk content was created and distributed on a *lot* of websites, for no other reason than to create more links back to sites they wanted to promote – for themselves or for their clients.

This is what we now refer to as "web SPAM."

Google put a stop to this with their Penguin update. The short, non-technical version of the message this update sent to the marketing world was that all content created *only* for the purpose of increasing the number of links back to sites they were promoting would no longer be acceptable.

And Google is now very good at finding them.

Fortunately, today, we know that it's not the *number* of links that plays a major role in where Google ranks your site, but the *quality* of those links.

No longer is more the same as better.

Concentrate, then, on creating specific types of high-quality content on your site, something that's useful to people. Share it everywhere and *some* people will naturally choose to link to it. These are the kinds of back-links you *want*.

One example of this kind of information, for me, is the calculators I have on my site. My lifetime value[3] and return on investment in your marketing[4] calculators are tools a lot of people like. They link to them, to share them with others. This gets me quality back-links that help my site's ranking in the search engines.

In some cases, a quality info-graphic can also generate a lot of links. They've become an extremely popular way to deliver quality content that's easy for people to grasp quickly.

Videos, eBooks, and other useful content can all result in quality back-links, but be careful you don't rely on them too heavily. A lot of web spammers still use them, too. Google could decide, at some point, to discount all of them, to maintain the overall quality of their listings. It's not imminent, or even necessarily likely, but the possibility's still there.

Game-change confirmed...

I watched a webinar that confirmed the game as we know it has been forever changed. The very smart team at Page One Power revealed the results of three companies' efforts to build links, in their attempt to rank highly for the keyword "HR Software."

---

[3] http://scottadennison.com/customer-lifetime-value-calculator/
[4] http://scottadennison.com/return-on-investment-calculator/

Jon Ball, CEO of Page One Power, was interested in finding out how many of the links these companies had were actually being counted by Google when ranking their pages.

The site ranked at number one had 38,452 back-links in their profile, but it was believed that only 447 of those were the high-quality, high-value links that actually improved their search rankings.

The number two website showed 17,364 links in their profile, but only 139 of those were being counted.

The site listed number three showed 331,516 (that's not a typo) links and, of these, there were only 181 that Google considered high-value.

Imagine focusing all the time, energy, and money that was required to create over 300,000 back-links, to find that only .0005 percent of them were helping you. The rest were the kind of SPAM that Google and other search engines *hate*.

So – what type of link-building *should* your teams be doing? Start with research. You want to find the high-value sites that are relevant to your ideal target customer's interests and see if they'll link to your site.

Looking closely at the link profile of your competitors might yield some clues to which high-value sites you want to get links from. Again, if your site offers a lot of high-quality useful content, people will be more inclined to link to you naturally.

It's kind of funny, really. When Google first hit the world with their Penguin update, you could almost *hear* the roars of frustration from the creators of all that web SPAM, now rendered pretty much useless. The funny thing is how incensed they are that Google caught on to their game and shut them down cold.

They should have been angry with themselves. Instead, many expressed their open displeasure with Google's decision about how it should run its own service.

Let's just say Google wasn't impressed. Penguin stands today, just as it did when they implemented it – along with some additional minor updates along the way.

Remember – Google and other search engines are a modern form of media. Like any magazine, newspaper, or broadcast, the search listings they deliver are the content they provide to the market. They want to deliver a high-quality experience to their users. Help them, and they'll reward you with leads and business. Work against them, and they'll destroy your business website's visibility without warning.

Social SEO aka: some special secret sauce for you...

Here's one many people fail to see. It's honestly the "secret sauce" to SEO success with your content, so pay close attention.

The search engines are also now able to see how often people engage with your excellent content. The number of "likes," "shares," re-tweets, blog comments, etc. that each of your content posts receives translates into social signals that are now factored into where your page appears in search results and where it's listed when it does.

For this reason, a part of the online lead generation process today involves developing and cultivating a following on one or more of the social media networks and sharing your content with them there.

When I share my articles with readers, I also make it a point to reply to those who take the time to comment, letting them know I want to build a connection with them.

Even if they just "like" a post, I'll send them a note and thank them for the "vote." Often, we end up following one another after that and they further engage with my information going forward.

The point: if search engines are measuring who likes your work enough to share it, comment on it, or to engage with you over it in some other way, then you have an excellent opportunity to gain visibility in the listings as you begin building relationships with the visitors.

In today's socially-connected online world, those relationships turn into leads and new business.

Do they *really* know their SEO?

Here's three ways to figure out which of the "SEO experts" you're now working with or talking to don't know what they're doing:

1) If they're talking about the need to build thousands of back-links to your site, because the guy who's listed number one has them. This just shows a limited understanding of what their *real* job is. It also makes it clear you need someone else to handle this task for you. If you can get just 10-15 high-quality sites to link to you this month – it's plenty. Just keep that up and you'll keep building your visibility as you go.

Remember…steady, consistent action gets the right kind of search engine attention.

2) If, when discussing link building, they use article marketing, "content spinning," or other similar "Google tricks." This is the epitome of the junk that Google's trying to remove from their index. If you or your team contributes to the junk pile, don't be too surprised if Google decides to punish you for it. This punishment can mean you might find your site listed on page 100 – where no one ever looks – if it's not banned from the listings altogether. It happens!

3) If they're still using bulk directory registrations or social media profiles as a way of getting links for your site. This demonstrates they still don't understand that it's *quality* Google is looking for – *not* quantity. Directory listings and social media profiles are excellent…but go easy and remain natural with it.

So – how *do* you choose the best SEO service?

When it comes to knowing who is the "best," that's subjective. The best is probably someone you like most and whose credentials check out. The one who is most accessible and available to help you when you need it most. The one who doesn't see the need to speak in riddles and then tell you its too complicated for you to understand.

Oddly enough, you'll select the best provider of this service the same way your new leads will decide they want to do business with you – *by finding someone you know, like, and trust.*

Coincidence? I think not!

> *By now, you've seen the power of properly earned back-links and you understand more fully what it is Google really wants – key factors in winning the SEO game. You also know how make social SEO sizzle and how to find the best professional SEO help possible, avoiding the worst. Now all you need to do is start tracking your results, to apply the 80/20 Rule and fine-tune everything. We'll cover that next.*

CHAPTER TEN

Checking Your Results

In this chapter, you will learn:
• How Google helps track results
• Why tracking matters
• Mapping the steps to more sales
• Less fools = more time off
• Making your goals reality

A combination of direct marketing with Internet lead generation makes tracking your results a fairly straightforward matter. Google analytics – a free tool Google provides – will show you all the traffic coming to each of your pages and where it came from. Your PPC campaign will show you the CTR for your paid campaigns.

This tracking makes it possible to know your conversion percentage, adjust your campaigns accordingly, and continually improve your results as you grow.

Your main concern, then, is starting with the right goal. Mapping out where you want to be, once you've made the necessary adjustments. This is how you know where you're currently located along the path to your goal.

Your goal is the gold...

Yesterday morning, as I finished getting myself all sweaty on the elliptical machine, the device flashed a message that said: "18:20 in the zone."

But – *what* zone would that be?

It's the fat burning and cardio zone.

That means, more than 90% of the time I was doing sprints on this machine, I was in the optimal zone for getting the result I want most.

Imagine structuring your sales day this way – where you're spending 90% of your time invested in getting the result you want most.

I think, if I were to sit down and walk through it with you, you'd say the result you want most is more sales.

It's a series of steps, just as my workout is. You have the goal in mind and all the tools you need to know the effectiveness of the steps you're taking to get there. It's not altogether different from tracking your progress working out at the gym.

So – more sales requires more leads, right?

To get more leads, you have to have more people looking at your business. To get more people looking at what you do, you have to have a system. For most, that system requires that you identify who your ideal customer or client is (your market) and then create and refine a message to deliver to your ideal market that speaks to their issues.

Finally, you need to communicate that message through a form of media that your ideal client or customer is looking at.

We've covered the steps pretty thoroughly. I'm repeating them here, to make certain you're with me so far. Do these things, and you'll have that system – one capable of producing the results you were looking for when you turned the first page of this book.

Even better, with the power of direct marketing for online lead generation, your future success moving forward is totally quantifiable. You can hold every piece of the system accountable as you proceed. Because you can measure the results, you also have the opportunity to improve them, little by little, until you get more of what you want or need, just as a pilot adjusts the flight path of a plane.

More leads. Increased sales. Higher profits.

Apply the 80/20 Rule to each step in the process, and to the results of the process as a whole, and the potential for growth in your business will quickly become unstoppable... controlled only by your willingness to do more.

Now that we're here – my challenge to you today is this:

Look at your calendar for the last week and figure out how much of your prime working hours were spent in selling situations with qualified prospects who can buy the products or services you offer.

If you're not at the 80% mark yet, don't worry – at least you'll know where you are now. That means you can improve and you know how much improvement is needed before you're there.

You're already in a far better situation than most business owners.

For example, I recently chatted with a business leader who's current marketing services provider is just beaming because he's now getting more than a dozen keywords ranked on page one of Google.

The problem is, the combined number of searches per month for all of those keywords is (wait for the drum roll)…10.

Meanwhile, my clients often average two-three new leads per *day*.

This can only happen when your business is ranked properly for the keywords your ideal client is using, to find solutions to the problems they have that you can solve. More important, this "visibility" creates traffic to your website and those visitors convert into leads at a *measurable* rate.

To track your progress with everything I've shown you so far, the 80-20 Rule is the key. Focus in on your keywords and the traffic you're attracting. Track your resulting leads (conversions) and sales (the whole reason we're doing all this). Look for the 20% of your keywords producing 80% of your results. They will be there. Drop the under-performers and test new ones.

The same goes for your PPC ads. And your customers.

Suffer less fools…enjoy more time off.

You have to start out with the right goal and the right attitude to make reaching that goal happen.

To this day, I still can't believe what I saw written down on a sheet of paper handed to me by a supposedly seasoned sales professional.

There it was, however – his stated goals:

1) Suffer less fools
2) Enjoy more time off

Here's the story:

I was training a group of car sales guys at a dealership near Los Angeles. My focus was better business and selling skills and a part of my training revolved around setting goals.

The reason I was there was to promote an upcoming seminar in Burbank, California, for the late Jim Rohn, and to invite sales teams from all over the Los Angeles area to invest in themselves, buy a ticket, and attend.

The worksheet I used made it easy for attendees of my training to take some notes and write responses to questions I was asking. However, in almost every case, the things someone wrote down would remain personal and private.

Except this once.

One of the men in attendance that day was clearly having a bad day. It's possible that he just had a bad attitude or something. He resented the fact that I was there and didn't want *anyone* telling him how to improve his results.

But, his bosses invited me there to share my information and the majority of those who sat in got value from what I had to offer.

Not *this* guy.

No.

When my presentation was done, some of the sales people who attended bought tickets to the program and some didn't. That's all completely normal. Then, the sales teams left the training room and got started on their day.

As I cleaned up and was preparing to leave, I saw one of the worksheets on the table – so I picked it up and began to read the notes.

I got to the section about goals and started laughing out loud.

This got the attention of both the sales manager and the General Manager of the dealership.

"What's so funny?" they asked.

When I showed the worksheet to them, neither responded with laughter. They looked at each other and I could tell they knew *exactly* who's handwriting they were looking at.

One said to the other, "I think we should help him accomplish his goals!"

So, the man was summoned to return to the training room, to confirm that this was his handwriting and these were his goals.

Yes. It was *that* guy.

He said, "But, but, but – I thought it was all a *joke!*"

The GM replied, "It wasn't. And we've decided that, today, you'll be able to accomplish *both* of your goals. You have 15 minutes to clear out your desk and leave the building."

Ouch! He *fired* the guy – right in front of me!

It's important to remember that written goals are powerful. Once you write them down, they start to become real for you – sometimes quicker than you thought possible.

Many business owners – possibly even you – don't have written goals. They go to work each day without a crystal clear sense of what their dream outcome is for their business.

Remember: You can't hit a goal that you don't have. And having no goal makes operating your business harder than it needs to be.

This is why I've hammered goal-setting and tracking your results throughout this book. You set a goal you should aim for. Write it down. Then, follow what I've shown you so far and track each step. You'll reach that goal. Probably faster than you ever thought would be possible.

Write down your goal. Track your progress. Simple.

I would never recommend that you simply throw your family into the car and head out for a vacation "somewhere." You'd be far better off selecting a destination, mapping out how to get there, then tracking your progress as you drive, taking each smaller required step along the way. Right?

Just do as much planning and tracking of your progress for your business as you would for a fine vacation and you'll find that your entire life is better for it.

Follow the steps I've outlined so far, track your progress, apply the 80-20 Rule to all the steps, and you'll find yourself approaching that sweet spot you're aiming for – plenty of solid prospects…the kind of people you most like working with and who generate the most profits for you when you do – much sooner than you could ever imagine you would.

So – I've gone through the entire process I follow for maximum lead generation online. I've shown you all the steps involved and how to carry them out. This chapter, I also showed you how to tap Google's amazing tracking capabilities and combine them with direct sales techniques on your site, to get more leads faster than you most likely thought was possible before. I've also shown you how to apply the 80/20 Rule to all of this, to stay on track and continually maximize your results. Next, we'll look at where you need to focus the bulk of your attention, to keep the leads coming into the foreseeable future. We'll also take a glance at what we can expect in the world of online lead generation as we move into the future.

Ongoing Considerations and the Future

> **In this chapter, you will learn:**
> - It's all about traffic and conversion
> - The forecast is straightforward
> - Content will continue to rule
> - SEO and PPC to keep on keepin' on
> - Social SEO will grow
> - Mobile considerations

Your next steps are clear, based on what we know today:

Maintain your focus on web traffic and conversions!

An old historian once wrote that *"Faith without works is dead."* Perhaps you've heard that said somewhere before, but I want to twist the expression a bit, so you can use it to help grow your business.

There is no trackable benefit to having traffic without converting as much of it to a buyer or subscriber, as quickly as possible. Get your conversions from traffic cooking and you'll see more traffic from better rankings just because you did. It can become exponential – not to mention addictive!

This is your number one ongoing concern for the foreseeable future.

You don't really need a crystal ball or extrasensory capabilities to see the future of online lead generation for business, to be honest. As I see it, things will likely escalate down the path they're currently cascading along. A reliance on web traffic to cost-effectively generate new business leads will definitely continue. I'm not talking about freeway-level web traffic here, mind you, but *real* web traffic...people who actually *visit* your web site.

The old "tricks" will continue to fail and new ones will pop up from time to time, only to be squashed and rendered useless, too. If you follow all the rules and are ranking organically – and appear at the top of the search results for an important keyword that people are searching, you can get a *lot* of ongoing traffic.

Still, if that traffic doesn't convert in some way, what do you *really* have?

One thing you *might* have is a significant bounce rate. I've defined this already, but here's how our friend, Wikipedia[5], describes it:

"Bounce rate (sometimes confused with exit rate) is an Internet marketing term used in web traffic analysis. It represents the percentage of visitors who enter the site and 'bounce' (leave the site) rather than continue viewing other

---

[5] http://en.wikipedia.org/wiki/Bounce_rate

pages within the same site. Bounce rate is a measure of the effectiveness of a website in encouraging visitors to continue with their visit."

A high bounce rate is *not* good. Google (and perhaps other search engines, too) now considers your bounce rate as a signal when deciding where to rank your site. It makes sense that if your web traffic leaves your site right away, you're most likely not giving your visitors what they expected to find. If that happens to a great degree, you won't be ranked at the top for long.

I see this trend continuing, along with other factors that will increasingly play a roll in the overall ranking system and SEO practices.

Quality, Relevant Content Is Key

Considering the growing importance such factors as your bounce rate already have in your success, it's no wonder perhaps the biggest change in SEO to come along in a *long* while has been an increased focus by the search engines on quality content directly related to the search listing that brings visitors to the page. This makes *quality* content now a *must*.

In the future, you can expect more changes in this area, all designed to make certain that the content being delivered is of highest possible quality. Also, don't rule out the addition of human rankings, at some point. Rather than a computer algorithm determining the position of your listing in the search results, these rankings will come from the human readers of your content themselves, through mechanisms similar to Facebook's "like" button and Google's "+".

I feel so certain of this I don't even consider it a prediction.

Because of this continued escalating reliance on the quality of the content being delivered for search results, you're already poised to stay on top of the game if you focus on its importance *right now*. Make quality content your priority. You won't be sorry you put in the extra effort or dollars to develop your content to the highest level possible.

One of the content marketing experts at the *Content Marketing Institute*, Katie McCaskey, recently filed a post[6] stating that content marketing was about to burst the "SEO web writing" bubble that's been growing for some time.

I completely agree with Katie's assessment. This is why, since the early part of the new century, I've been positioned and working as a content marketing expert.

Content marketing experts – especially the ones with integrity – will tell you that, if your website content has the basic on-page factors met, and the content is good enough to share with others, the SEO will pretty much take care of itself.

Therefore, focus on the content.

As Katie said in her post, "The search engines are wising up, and so are the people embracing content marketing." Keep

---

[6] http://www.contentmarketinginstitute.com/2011/01/content-marketing-seo/

this simple truth in mind as you employ a strategy that will increase your visibility in search results.

My suggestion? Have content marketing experts on your team, develop a content marketing strategy and watch your site grow and prosper.

Will SEO still be important?

Considering all these changes, should you still be focusing on and investing in SEO? Absolutely! It's just becoming evermore apparent that tricks won't cut it. Increasingly, they can get you de-listed or demoted to Google's "back pages," where no one who isn't your own mother will find you.

There were lots of moans and complaints when Google started enforcing their rules against web spam and link manipulation. Unfortunately for the whiners, this game will continue to change because – let's face it – *it's Google's game.* They can change it any way they wish.

You probably see your listing on Google as free advertising for your business. Google sees it differently. To Google, your listing is the content they deliver that attracts people to their search engine. Their search engine is, essentially, their publication. They make their money selling advertising in that publication...but the rates they can charge for that advertising – and the number of advertisers they can attract – are based on the number of visitors Google can attract to their content.

So far, they've done a better-than-fair job of attracting a lot of "readers" to their content, primarily because of their relentless focus on providing quality results for the searches those readers perform.

Provide Google the content they're looking for and they'll feature it for you. Free.

It's a good deal and it's one I think we can count on being available to us for a long time to come. However, we also need to be more realistic about what Google's *really* up to, what they *really* want, and work harder to give them exactly that. The punishment for not "getting it" will be worse in the future…not better.

Believe it or not, there's still widespread belief that you can get to the top of search results simply by having more links than your competitor. Even if this were true, it's short-term thinking. Google's total devotion to improving the quality of their search results, their computing power, and their money enables them to eventually stop *any* link manipulation cold.

If your site is sitting on top of search results because of tricks, consider it a temporary situation. Google *will* one day – later if not right away – change that.

So – yes, you should definitely continue to focus on SEO moving into the future. This is, however, conditional. There are a couple of caveats:

First – you must have at least a basic understanding of what does and does not work today.

Today, SEO is still largely limited to your "on-page" factors, which are your title tags, meta description tags, header tags, and such. Get these right and you're way ahead of the game now and going into the future.

Second – *some* links are important.

Getting high-value sites to link to your site can definitely help you. But, this needs to be very selective and done very carefully. *The volume of links to your site is not important. The quality of links to your site is – and will be even more so as we move forward.*

The bottom line? If you want to get more traffic to your site, being found higher in search results is *one* way to do that. SEO can be a part of how that's accomplished, and quality relevant content is clearly a path to reaching this goal that will continue to gain in importance.

I believe it's vitally important, however, to have a proven model in place for converting that traffic into leads. Once you do, you can generate traffic to your site from a variety of places, including – but not limited to – SEO. You'll also get more back-links when your content is worthy of sharing, and people will hang around your site, instead of bouncing away the moment they hit it.

The importance of another key web traffic source – paid advertising – will continue to grow.

This is big and getting bigger because, finally, people are waking up to the "real" cost of web traffic. *With social and organic/SEO traffic, you often pay by investing hours and hours of your time to make it work.* With paid advertising, such as PPC ads on Facebook, LinkedIn, or Google, you pay by writing a check and you only invest a small amount of time to see very fast, trackable results.

Perhaps the real upside of paid advertising is that there's no limit to how much traffic you can generate. If you can convert that web traffic into something that leads to income for you, PPC can be the kick-starter to more leads you were looking for. Otherwise, you'll end up with a huge credit card bill and a massive headache.

Again, the key here is top-notch quality, *relevant* content to which you drive your PPC traffic, on pages specifically designed to focus on one thing: getting a visitor to convert, either as a buyer or as a subscriber to a list.

What about social media as a source of web traffic?

I know that about half of my current traffic, in some weeks, now comes from the content I share on social media – mostly from LinkedIn. This site continues to gain respect and power in the world of business-to-business social media. Facebook and Google+ both offer business pages, but they've never gained the traction with business "insiders" that LinkedIn has and I believe things will stay this way for at least a while yet.

I'm not saying we won't see Google+ continue to gain its own relevance on the social media scene, however. Google continues to add new functions and features to its own social platform and it certainly has the means to continue developing more. Since Google+ is also *directly* tied to Google in ways no other social media sites outside of YouTube can be, the service certainly should be included in any SEO and lead generation efforts now and into the near future.

Likewise, YouTube has gotten more social. Google has not only connected YouTube to its Google+ social networking platform, it's also adding features that allow people to connect and share videos more easily on YouTube, among other functions. Given the fact that this site, too, is owned by Google, it's also most certainly favored by Google search. I expect to see its capabilities and power for rankings and overall visibility for business grow as time passes. Consider getting some videos on YouTube as part of your strategy now and start building a following.

Somewhere along the way, Google added social interaction to the list of things it considers in search rankings. This is when the concept of "social SEO" was born.

SOCIAL SEO WILL BECOME INCREASINGLY IMPORTANT AS WE MOVE INTO THE NEAR FUTURE.

~ Scott A. Dennison

I see social SEO becoming increasingly important as we move into the near future.

In hindsight (as in: I wish I'd thought of that in time to make a billion or two), it makes sense. When trying to score millions of pages, to figure out which ten are the most relevant for any given search term, you'd want to look at the page itself (on-page optimization[7]), the back-links that point to that page (off-page optimization[8]), and how readers *engage* with the content.

To track this, you would ask, "Do they stick around and read it (making time on-site and bounce rates a factor) – and do they share it with others?"

Facebook "likes," Twitter "tweets," LinkedIn "shares" and, of course, Google's "+1," are all being factored into the search results now. These and 190 or so other "signals" are considered in what ranks where in search engine results pages today.

To say it's complicated is an understatement. To make it all happen in less than one second is a technological miracle. The only thing stopping Google from taking it to the next unimaginable step right now is the time it takes to develop that next step...and they're most likely already working on it.

Still, it's a safe bet to guess that Google's focus on Social SEO will continue to grow in importance, especially since it's in social SEO where the seeds of human rankings for content will be found lurking.

This makes it a great idea to master social SEO right now. Doing so requires that you create good – if not great – content.

---

[7] http://scottadennison.com/learn-on-page-seo/
[8] http://scottadennison.com/how-to-build-backlinks/

Since the idea of "great" is subjective, at best, there are some things you can do, to help yourself rank better.

5 Keys To Successful Social SEO

Let's run through five things you can do, starting today, to improve your social SEO:

Write the best content you can. Do a bit of research, link out to authoritative sources – and make sure you've spelled everything correctly. If you're outsourcing your writing, make sure content published in your name is written by someone who writes and speaks your native language. There are endless examples of articles written by foreign writers that are essentially unreadable. Believe me when I say such content won't rank well.

Be sure to provide social sharing buttons in your post or on your page. If you're using WordPress, there are many free plugins that can help your social SEO by making it easy for visitors to share your information with others.

Encourage comments on your post. If you want to build a following, ask people to add their opinions and join in the conversation yourself when they do.

Share the content to your social following. Just about everyone has a Facebook profile and many have a Facebook page[9] – share your content there. If you have a Twitter account, be sure to tweet out the link to your article or page. If

---

[9] http://facebook.com/howtogetmoreclients

you're on LinkedIn, share it in the groups you participate in and, of course, if you're a Google + user, post it there as well. The magic happens when friends of your followers engage with your information, too. It can then quickly spread, far and wide.

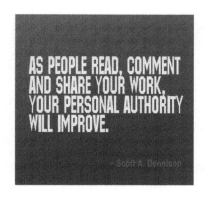

Automate the sharing of your content. There are some incredible tools that can automate some of the work involved in sharing your work. One that I like and use is called If This, Then That[10]. This nifty free tool uses "recipes" to take the content you're adding to your website and share it automatically to various places.

If you do nothing more than these five things, in combination with the other elements we've discussed in this book, your social SEO scores will begin to improve.

As people read, comment, and share your work, your personal authority will improve, too. The result of that is more people who want or need what your business provides who will see you "out there" and begin to think of you as an expert. When everything

---

[10] http://ifttt.com/

else is equal, people will choose to do business with an expert, so why not *become* that expert?

Everything is Going Mobile

I mentioned the Who earlier, and how one of their songs rolls through my head every time I start honing in on who exactly a client is, in the eyes of their very best customers. Oddly enough, there's a second song of theirs I hear almost as often – the lesser-known, "Going Mobile."

Before you start thinking it must be really weird inside my head (and, honestly, sometimes it can get that way), I'd better get to the point: in personal computing, *everything's* going mobile. Mobile computing has been gradually overtaking desktop and laptop PCs for the past decade and we're at that sweet spot right now where things have tipped. Mobile computing devices are dominating.

More and more people are looking at your website and pages on smaller screens these days. This is where using WordPress to develop your web pages *really* comes in handy. When you select a theme to put your content into on WordPress, make sure that theme is described as "responsive." Responsive pages automatically notice visitors coming in from a mobile device and adjust the screen and layout of your page to better accommodate them.

You also want to make certain you're ranking in SEO for local terms, if your business is primarily local in nature. Adding your city and state to the terms you rank on makes it far easier to rank on top of terms that might otherwise be overcrowded nationwide. This also signals your location to mobile users who might just drop by while they're already out in your area.

Mobile's influence on everything is rapidly becoming the norm. We can expect this trend to continue for some time yet. Software applications, online and offline – and even computer operating systems – are increasingly moving to "chiclet"-style graphics, designed to be easier to see and manipulate on smaller touch-sensitive screens. There will definitely be more of this as mobile's dominance grows over the next few years.

Adding a "push to call us" button on your site (a simple process with a WordPress plugin to do so) is also recommended, as most mobile devices these days are also phones. If a prospect can easily find you in search, then simply tap a chiclet to call you instantly, you'll see better results, don't you think?

Today's forecast calls for...

This a.m., while getting my sweat on, I glanced at the TV in the gym and started laughing out loud.

You know how, especially on news or sports channels, they have those scrolling bands of content along the bottom of the screen? This is where they tell you all the headlines of stories they're not currently reporting on.

Oftentimes, there are two or more such bands of info, each reporting something or another.

So – I looked up and, in a large bold print, it said, "Today's Forecast."

Below that, scrolling from left to right, it said, "A car accident with injuries on the Veterans Expressway."

I think I'd want to avoid that road today, if they're able to forecast such a thing.

On a more serious note, today's weather is often quite easy to predict. If you're in Florida and it's summer, it's going to be hot – like, in the 90's – with a chance of afternoon showers. If you're in California, it's usually sunny and warm, with low humidity.

With exceptions for storm systems that show up here and there, the weather forecast is often very similar to what it was yesterday.

And so it is, too, with most businesses marketing.

It's often almost identical to what it was yesterday, last week, last month and, sometimes, even last year.

The results of said marketing?

All too often, it's also the same.

That can be a good thing – or it can be a bad thing, too.

The point is this:

I've done my best, given what I've seen through the years and dealt with regularly in my own dealings with numerous business owners, to give you a glimpse into the future of online lead generation. The goal was to let you know best what you need to be doing now, to continue growing your business with new leads into the foreseeable future.

However…like those weather predictions, except for a few unexpected storms here and there (a totally unanticipated introduction of a new type of software or online service useful for marketing, for example), things will pretty much stay the same. What's popular and growing right now will pretty much stay growing. What isn't will increasingly get slapped down.

Note the differences and act accordingly.

The keys to creating a bright future for your business.

If your pattern is to market your business aggressively, targeting those you think would be ideal prospects, and…

If you lead with an understanding of what the prospect's needs are, and…

If you tie your USP and guarantees to their wants and needs…

…things are probably going to be pretty decent for you, results-wise.

You see, if you aren't really clear on who an ideal prospect might be, if you're not speaking to what their wants and needs are, and if you fail to offer anything in your marketing to communicate that *you* are unique, then many, if not most, of your opportunities will be based on your willingness to sell for less money than your competitor will.

Something to think about, yo?

The future, then, is bright for SEO and online lead generation and it's bright for you – *if* you consistently follow and apply what I've shown you in this book.

That's a forecast that makes me smile.

> *There you have it. Online lead generation done right. You now know enough to get your own going in the right direction – or to intelligently hire the help you need to get it done. And you know how important it is. You also have a grasp of what to expect in the near future. Apply what I've shared here and it will be a bright future for you. That's precisely why I do what I do for a living and I would love seeing nothing else.*

Conclusion

You know by now that I work out pretty regularly. Staying fit is one of my goals. Oddly enough, I see marketing lessons in everything and, because I spend time at the gym, several come from there.

Recently, I was at the fitness club when I looked up and saw a man wearing a t-shirt that said, "Nobody trains to make excuses."

Interesting.

But true.

I'm pretty sure it's true because excuse-making seems to come naturally for so many people. This most likely explains why I've never seen anyone offering classes in better excuse-making.

If such a course was available, there'd probably be *lines* of people who wanted to master this as a skill going around the block. Even business owners – the *last* people who should be making excuses – often show the most creativity in coming up with the reasons for not owning their results.

Ever heard this one? "Well…the competition is ____."

Or this one? "My customers ____."

You can fill in the blanks with whatever excuse you might think that fits. I've heard 'em all.

I'm not going to suggest that I've never done it – or that the disease is ever fully cured in any of us, but there *are* some truths that will help you make today's results better than yesterday's.

One is that you (and I) are 100% responsible for what happens to us. We're responsible for our marketing, who it attracts, and how prospects respond to it.

I was fortunate to have a manager many years ago who beat the heck out of me verbally whenever I offered an excuse for not closing the sale on an appointment he'd sent me on.

Gary believed that I was so well prepared and the leads were so well qualified that no reason (another term for excuse) was acceptable for not closing the deal.

So – what about you?

Do you tend to offer (or accept) excuses when you don't get the type of customers you want? Or when they don't buy?

Stop. Today.

I can encourage you to own your results, but the truth is you have to be the one to say, "enough!"

You now know that your ideal customer should be your focus. Knowing precisely who this is enables you to constantly direct your message to that person in the media he or she is using most often today – and to know which media that would be.

You already know the steps. Direct marketing makes all the difference in making online lead generation the powerful business builder it can be.

You also now know how all of this is measurable throughout the process, utilizing the 80-20 Rule, to keep a laser focus on your course as you move along. This makes you capable of quick small adjustments that keep you on track to growing returns, just as a pilot stays on course with tiny adjustments to the entire flight path, to reach a destination.

We've gone over setting up your SEO and optimizing your company website for lead generation and acquisition. And we've covered the power of PPC, to get your online lead generation on a fast track to results.

I've taken you through the steps. You can take them as far as you're willing to go. But, you need to set that destination, then make a plan that will serve as your roadmap for reaching it.

Don't underestimate the power of a plan.

And don't feel bad if you've failed to plan adequately before now.

About a year ago, I started a poll in several of my LinkedIn groups and asked: "Does your business have a detailed, written marketing plan?"

My local Chamber of Commerce had reported that about 75% of their member businesses didn't have a marketing plan. I was trying to verify (or debunk) those numbers, because they sounded far-fetched to me.

You see, having worked with some of these businesses and having a seat on the business education committee, I got to see up close what happens when a business operates without a plan.

It's rarely pretty.

"If you fail to plan, you're planning to fail."

That quote, often repeated in business everywhere, originated with businessman, author, and speaker, Harvey Mackay.

It's as true in this case as it was when he originally said it.

It's my view that many things can go wrong, whether you have a plan or not. When you don't have a plan in place to guide your marketing, however, you can't ever really know if your plan is working or it isn't.

We'll look at three things that can go wrong in just a bit. You can judge for yourself whether having a plan would help or not from there.

First, you might be interested in what my survey revealed. While only a small sample responded, I feel the numbers would hold up with a larger number of responses.

In my poll I found that:

25% DO NOT HAVE a marketing plan

70% DO have a detailed, written marketing plan

5% DON'T KNOW if they have a marketing plan

Obviously, the numbers I got came out quite different from the numbers reported by the local Chamber. Perhaps some of the respondents answered "yes," but did so out of ego, when they don't actually have a written plan.

To be clear, I'm not advocating that we break out a dusty copy of *Marketing 101* and approach this like your old college Professor told you to. Remember – many who teach marketing at the university level have never actually *done* any marketing themselves.

Unless you run a huge business, there's almost no need to do such things as a SWOT analysis (**side note:** If you don't know what that is – don't worry, most business owners don't).

Still, as encouraging as my own numbers were, you have to ask: "Why don't *all* business owners have a marketing plan?"

One of my respondents commented that, "I think most small business owners are completely overwhelmed as it is and, when you throw the word 'marketing plan' at them, they just freeze up."

That could be the case. If you don't have a plan at all, however, then it's likely that one or more of these three things are currently affecting your business success *negatively*:

1) You don't know *who* your ideal customer is, therefore you end up attracting *any* customer – even ones you don't want.

2) You don't know the lifetime value of an ideal customer, so it's impossible to know how much you should invest to attract one.

3) You're subject to buying advertising from the next ad sales rep who walks through your door, because you have no strategic filters in place to determine if the advertising you buy will produce a respectable ROI.

Each of these can be avoided with the right planning.

First, if you don't know *who* your ideal customer is and you end up serving anyone and everyone, you can't strategically grow. We've all served the "wrong" customers before, right?

Most of you would probably admit these type of customers were harder to please and consumed more resources than you budgeted for, which resulted in a low-margin sale, or even one where you lost money.

That's obviously *not* a great path to growth.

If you're strategic in your pursuit of ideal customers/clients, this happens a *lot* less often.

Next, when you don't know the lifetime value of your ideal customer, it's impossible to decide what you'll spend to attract one of them.

Look, growing your business is about *acquiring* customers[11] and then *keeping* them, hopefully for years to come.

When you plan to acquire customers through marketing, how are you supposed to know what you'd be willing to pay to get one, if you don't know what one is worth to you, long-term, after you do?

That seems more like a Vegas approach to business. Betting on black, so to speak.

In fact, one commenter on my poll – Marissa Brown – said: "One of the biggest benefits of a marketing plan – particularly for small businesses, where the owner traditionally wears many hats – is to ensure that any potential marketing activity is in line with your big picture goals for the business."

Yes, Marissa. You got it *exactly* right!

Which provides the perfect segue into the third point on that list…

You're at the mercy of the selling skills of your local advertising rep.

If a salesperson is talented and comes through your door to pitch you on a radio, TV, or print buy, you might just go for it. If they want you to paint your name on a bus bench, you might just say, "Sure!" Run a big ad in the phone book? You might say, "Ok." Run a coupon on a pizza box? "Why not?"

---

[11] http://scottadennison.com/need-to-get-more-customers-its-impossible-without-this/

This is the "you'll do" syndrome I discussed before and it's to be avoided at *all* costs.

I don't know who you are or what your current financial situation might be, but I'll assume the amount you're able to budget for marketing is finite. This is how it is with the clients I work with regularly. Even if your source of funds seems unlimited, it's insanity to throw down money on marketing with no idea what the ROI will be.

If its not producing an ROI, then you constantly have to invest new dollars in marketing with a diminishing return to keep the ball rolling – and success is a crap shoot at best.

Maybe someone will tell you you're investing in "branding." That it'll all "take off" *sometime.*

Maybe soon.

That's a lot of "power of branding" nonsense. Small businesses will *never, ever* be able to afford the real-world cost to "own a corner of the prospect's mind," which is Wikipedia's definition of branding.

Operating with a simple, but effective direct marketing online lead generation plan is a lot smarter (and more profitable).

Seriously – do this right and the only thing standing between the success you're aiming for and you…is *you.*

What BS!

Seriously. At this point, the *one* thing left that can stand in your way is – BS.

Recently, I had conversations with two gentlemen who both make their living in professional sales. In fact, both of them sell the same basic product line – but for different companies.

Their industry is fairly regulated, so both are dealing with all the rules, regulations, and similar "stuff" that goes on in their field.

One has a calendar that's maxed out. He's writing business all day, every day. The other is focused on the chaos in his marketplace and admits he's struggling.

What's the difference?

BS.

Now – before you get your exercise by jumping to conclusions about what I mean here – let me say it's probably not what you think.

However, if you and I were to talk a while, I'd probably discover that you have some BS that's preventing you from achieving all that's possible for you right now, too.

I'd even venture to say, if the tables were turned and you examined me closely, you'd find BS in my life that contributes to my outcomes, too.

I'm referring to **_Belief Systems_**. Something which, contrary to popular belief, is totally within your control.

We all have them and they dictate much of our success (or failure) each and every day that we're doing what we do.

Here's one that affects many of us: "I lost the sale today, because our prices are too high."

That's BS in action.

I'll submit to you that the number of people who actually make a buying decision based on the lowest price alone is extremely small. The only time it really happens is when everything else is equal. _Then_ price becomes an issue.

Your marketing and your positioning _all_ play a part in how people perceive what you're doing. This directly affects the results you're getting, at whatever price you're charging.

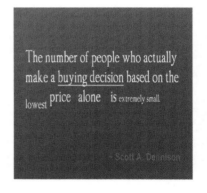

The number of people who actually make a buying decision based on the lowest price alone is extremely small.

— Scott A. Dennison

The man I mentioned earlier – the one who demonstrates a lack of confidence in his products and services and thinks the marketplace is the reason he's not doing well – is being crushed by his own BS.

You now have the information you need to break yourself free of that kind of thinking forever.

Excellent marketing changes all of that.

One of the secrets I discussed in this book was using content to get people familiar with your name – so they get to know you. Then, when you share quality content consistently and engage with your readers every chance you get, they begin to like and trust you.

This is when you have the chance – and maybe even the right – to proceed, looking for ways to monetize your relationships by turning followers and fans into serious prospects for your products and services.

And you now understand the power of sending social signals that let search engines know how important your content is.

With just these tips and some effort on your part, you can start to increase dramatically the number of people who find your business on search engines. When you implement a process to convert those visitors to leads, you have an opportunity to increase both your sales *and* profits.

I'll take the liberty here of assuming you're ready to do some marketing. Good for you!

I offer these four recommendations as you begin the process…consider it your shorthand bullet list of the steps:

Recommendation #1: Make a commitment to learn who your ideal client or customer is and then learn everything you can about them.

Perhaps most important thing in this process is to discover what the lifetime value of your customer is.

When you're armed with this information, you can make smart decisions about how to attract them.

Recommendation #2: List your objectives before investing in new marketing. When measuring successful marketing campaigns, be clear with yourself what success looks like *to you*. Most important, if you bring in help, look for a marketing partner who understands how important ROI is in your decision-making process, for the type of marketing you'll be using.

Recommendation #3: Ask *lots* of questions of anyone you choose to help you with your marketing! The best way to learn about a company is to ask specific questions and listen carefully to their response. If they're speaking buzzwords or confusing terms, insist that they speak to you in plain English and explain what they're talking about.

Here are some questions I suggest you ask, to make sure you're working with someone who deserves your business because they have what it takes to deliver the new leads to your doorstep that you need:

1. What types of marketing do you have experience with and which do you usually recommend?
2. Can you give me examples of successes you've had in working with other businesses? Why did these campaigns succeed?
3. Can you give me examples of campaigns you've done that failed? Why did they fail?

4. What type of training do you have in small business marketing? How often do you get continuing education and what type training?

Recommendation #4: Once you're satisfied with the responses and feel you're speaking with an honest, competent professional who can help you, invite them to develop a set of recommendations and provide you with a firm quote for the service they propose, *in writing*. A written proposal assures you of what the job will cost and what's involved. It also eliminates any surprises.

By following these four recommendations, you'll get all the information you need to make an informed, intelligent decision.

This won't lead you to the lowest-priced help available. It might even lead you to decide you want to try doing some of this yourself, first. It *will* lead you to the best value for your dollar possible.

Remember: if all you want is low-budget essentially ineffective marketing, many companies will be happy to take your money.

If, however, you want marketing that positions your small business effectively in front of your ideal prospective client or customer, attracting them into your business in the most cost-effective way – then I invite you to contact me. There are a number of ways you can do that coming right up next!

Resources

Visit my web site at http://scottadennison.com/8020-resources/ to access a number of tools, videos and additional training to help you increase the number of leads you're generating in your business from the Internet.

Check out my Customer Lifetime Value Calculator and my Return on Investment Calculator. These will help you determine some of the important numbers you'll need in your Internet based direct response marketing.

Subscribe for regular DIY online marketing and lead generation tips by email – all 100% free.

I've also developed a low cost training for entrepreneurial business leaders and their teams to build a rock solid marketing plan. If you don't have a solid marketing plan, or if the plan you have needs to be revised, I invite you to check out Marketing Plan Profits.

About the Author

I help roofing contractors[12] and other entrepreneurial business leaders – including attorneys, cosmetic dentists, chiropractors and plastic surgeons – achieve marketplace domination through effective Internet marketing lead generation.

I've been working online since 1998 when I launched my first technology company. I've helped dozens of companies achieve their online goals, which makes it possible for them to achieve their personal life passions.

In 2012, I authored my first web-based course, *NO Vacancy*[13], that taught Hotel owners how to effectively use Google Places to sell more hotel room nights.

In 2013, I created *Marketing Plan Profits*[14], to serve the many businesses that lack a marketing plan to serve as a foundation for their campaigns.

I've written hundreds of blog posts and eBooks and presented at marketing conferences all over the US.

My proprietary Marketplace Domination method is so powerful that companies who hire me generate hundreds of targeted, high-quality leads from their Internet marketing and grow their sales and profits exponentially.

---

[12] http://scottadennison.com/
[13] http://scottadennison.com/no-vacancy-google-places-course/
[14] http://scottadennison.com/marketing-plan-profits/

Made in the USA
San Bernardino, CA
07 February 2016